TEXTILE

DESIGNERS

AT THE CUTTING EDGE

For Ingrid and Jan

LAURENCE KING

Published in 2009
by Laurence King Publishing Ltd
361–373 City Road
London EC1V 1LR
Tel +44 20 7841 6900
Fax +44 20 7841 6910
E-mail enquiries@laurenceking.com
www.laurenceking.com

A catalogue record for this book is
available from the British Library.

ISBN 978 1 85669 581 7

Designed by Charlotte Heal

Picture Editor: Laya Saludo Sweeney

Printed in China

TEXTILE DESIGNERS

AT THE CUTTING EDGE

BRADLEY QUINN

Laurence King Publishing

CONTENTS

INTRODUCTION

Shredded selvedges, hand-stitched surfaces and woven textures may be the hallmarks of traditional textiles, but in the hands of contemporary designers, these craft techniques signify the fabrics of the future. And while the next generation of textiles is heralded by technological interfaces, programmable surfaces and architectonic capabilities, paradoxically they harken back to an age when woven fibres provided dwellings, sources of communication and manifestations of power. As they forged indissoluble links between architecture, dress, individuals and communities, textiles were literally the fabric of society.

Textiles have always held the promise of the future. We rarely remember that woven fibres were a technological breakthrough for early man, and easily forget their radical past as sources of progress and emblems of rebellion. I had, until I realized that the important roles they play in today's fast-moving times make them as indispensable now as they were five thousand years ago. Today's fashions, vehicles, interior textiles, communication technologies and cutting-edge architecture all consist of fibrous forms; although humanity has advanced dramatically, simple textile forms have carried us every step of the way.

Against this background, textile's engagement with product design, contemporary architecture and sources of technological innovation are hardly surprising – yet, the hybrid forms that result are still revolutionary. Although such collaborations mark an exciting moment in textile practice, this book was written to chart their significance to the wider discipline of design. As *Seamless* explores the work of 36 multi-disciplinary textile designers from approximately 16 countries around the world, their sources of inspiration and treatment of materials are explained in their own words. I've allocated the designers to the general categories of 'Body' or 'Space' to reflect the area in which they are best known, but it's worth bearing in mind that many are active in both.

New narratives unfolded as the designers provided unexpected insights into the cultures they come from and the markets for which they produce work. In Nordic countries such as Denmark and Finland, for example, where winters are long and dark, light was a source of inspiration for designers who decided to create illuminating textiles. Swedish designers told me how their clients are fashioning their homes rather than just decorating them, sparking a demand for fashion-conscious textiles that are as bespoke as any couture garment. German fashion designers described a similar phenomenon, where exchanges between clothing and other cultural forms are seamlessly integrating fashion and fabric design. They believe that today, neither is possible without the other.

In the Netherlands, textiles are forging new relationships with architecture and landscape design, enabling the boundaries between the three disciplines to fold into one another. British designers are pioneering a similar approach, albeit on a smaller scale. Shifting their focus from a fabric's surface to its structure, they are crafting a unique breed of structured textiles, which are often based on new sources of sustainable materials. Textile designers in India claim that recycling is nothing new; recent regeneration projects are merely contemporary expressions of traditions that have been around for thousands of years. As these designers transform trash into textiles, they reveal the power that the fabric industry has to regenerate the urban landscape and improve individual lives.

This book examines the changing face of textile design, it charts the furthermost boundaries of what a textile can be. As recent developments in the field of textiles present new technical possibilities, their applications in fashion, architecture and interior design have redefined them as a uniquely multi-disciplinary field of innovation and research. As today's textiles change how the human body is experienced and how the urban environment is built, they reveal their capacity to transform our world dramatically.

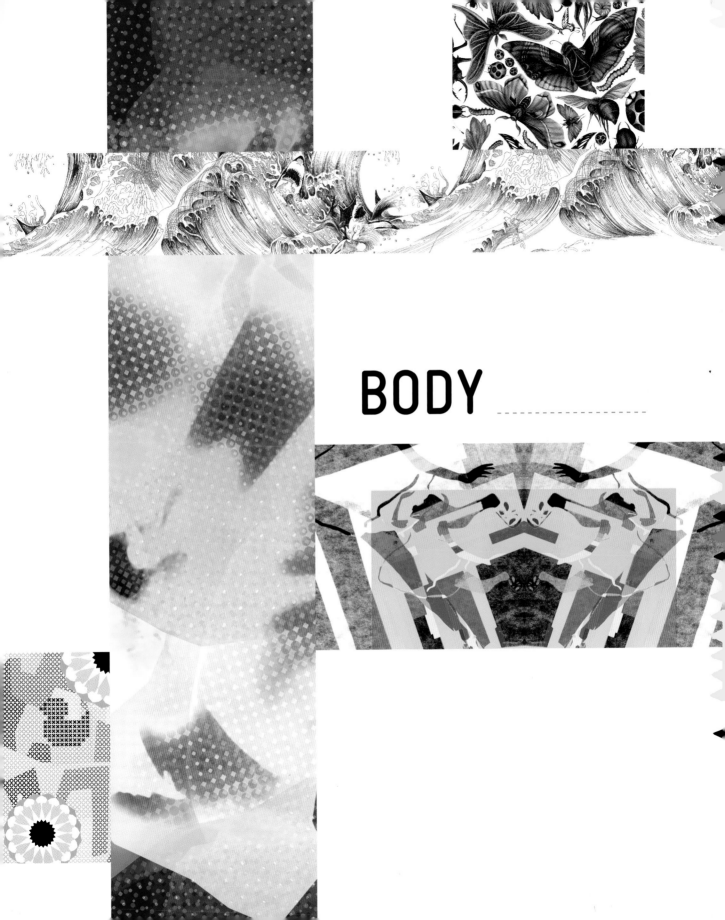

BODY

FABRIC AS SECOND SKIN

The garments tracing the surface of the body are often considered to be second skins, and the patterns covering them always say something about the wearer. Just as signs and symbols are easy to decode, patterns and motifs can also be (cunningly) deciphered. Or so I thought. These days, when fashion patterns glow, fade or disappear altogether, they probably tell us more about the future than they do about the present.

Thermochromatic dyes and UV-activated motifs are a popular choice for designers today, who produce fabrics for uncomplicated clothes with an edgy, urban style. Heat-sensitive repeats disappear on areas where textiles touch the body, then return to view once the garment has changed position. Similarly, photochromatic motifs are invisible in the dark, only surfacing when the pigments in them become exposed to UV light. Fashion textiles are moving forward so dramatically today that the synergy between textile designers and technology promises to transform the fashioned body forever.

But while many designers are pioneering the textiles of the future, others are cleaning up the mess left behind. The millions of tonnes of textiles buried in landfills each year was an industry secret for several decades, until textile designers began to address the growing problem of post-consumer waste. Some have come up with methods of re-cycling the millions of garments that are worn for one season and cast off when trends move forward. Many others are finding ways to transform discarded industrial fabrics into textiles that are as beautiful as they are sustainable, making sure that the processes used to recycle them minimize water pollution and chemical waste.

The passion for sustainable textiles has reclaimed organic materials and has resulted in contemporary expressions for many traditional crafts. In some cases, whole communities have been regenerated by forming artisan co-operatives and traditional textile workshops. Although contemporary fashion may be married to technology, it has not divorced craft skills completely. Embroidery, appliqué, beading and hand-stitching are as popular now as hi-tech prints and smart fabrics. Today, these two design cycles work side-by-side; as they reveal the economic and environmental value of recycled resources, they show a renewed respect for the artistry required to produce beautiful textiles.

ALEX
► RUSSELL

The love affair started in the spring of 1980. An emerging British designer, then aged 13, became besotted by screen-printing and soon started designing fabric prints and T-shirt motifs. The two broke up, at which point Russell embarked on a reckless fling with electronic engineering. Eventually, he was seduced by an art foundation course, which was what finally united Alex Russell with his true love: textile design. 'It seemed to combine all the things I liked best about the creative process,' he remembers. 'It's great that textile design now includes digital technology too, although drawing and colour remain absolutely central to what I do.'

Thank goodness Russell was only half in love; today, his designs are more likely to be sketched out on paper or created digitally than they are screen-printed. 'I really miss screen-printing,' he says, 'and if I could change something about the way I work today that's what I'd like to change. I'm always interested in finding out about new technology in design and I've started to produce designs specifically for digital printing. I'm also experimenting with digital design processes, but I'd love to be able to work with screen-printing on a regular basis.'

Russell thinks that digital printing will become more prevalent in the future and is excited about the impact this could have on repeat and colour use. However, he says, 'design increasingly becomes about selection, not creation, which is not necessarily a good thing. In future, consideration or disregard of environmental and social responsibilities will become increasingly important, meaning that companies and consumers are becoming more polarized. And as emerging economies develop their own design talent, designers in Western Europe face more competition.'

Commenting on whether the number of men in textile design is increasing, Russell thinks any perceived shift does not represent a real change. 'Male students on textile design courses are still outnumbered about ten to one by their female counterparts,' he says, 'but a greater proportion of men are running the bigger studios and hence getting the exposure. Right now, there's a trend for textile companies to collaborate with designers from fields like graphic design, which are more likely to be men. These designers tend to be credited by name for what they do, whereas textile designers, who are more probably women, generally remain uncredited for their work.'

Russell's studio was established to attract fashion and interiors clients (including Almedahls, Eco Tapeter, Lee, Levi Strauss, Moschino, Oilily, Roberto Cavalli, Speedo and Tommy Hilfiger), and he mainly works with Dutch studio Amsterstampa. 'I probably do more work for fashion than for interiors, but I really like both,' he says. 'I do printed textile design, surface patterns, graphics and illustrations. It's a bit of a mouthful, but probably more professional than describing myself as "does colouring-in".' For Russell, the future seems to be coloured in with a kaleidoscope of vibrant projects. Reflecting on his future directions, Russell describes three things that will continue to inspire his work: 'Things that look like nothing I've ever seen before, things that look like everything I've ever seen before, and things I wish I'd thought of myself.'

Alex Russell gives traditional floral designs a contemporary update as he overlays them with graphic patterns and geometric motifs. The plant forms that result are hybrids of digital technology and organic forms. | 1&3

Emblems of punk rebellion are featured in this graffiti-like print, making a comment on urban style. Clashing a vivid colour against a muted background is a hallmark of his work. | 2

3

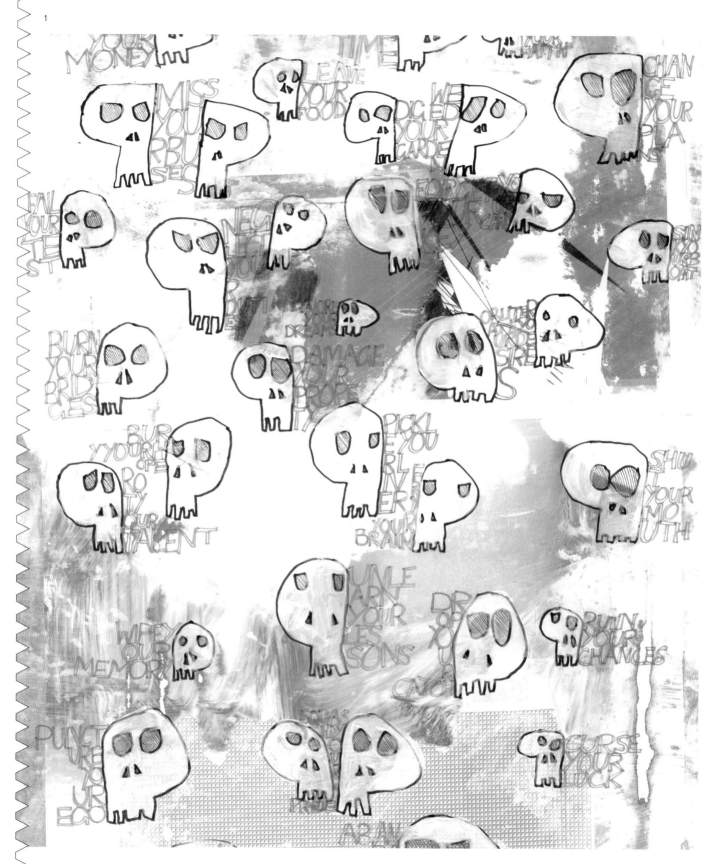

2

1 | Teenage rebellion is made tangible in this witty motif as Russell's maxims reassure youth – and adults – that they are allowed to make mistakes.

2 | This abstract landscape seems closer to contemporary art than textile design. Here, birds flying in a summer sky morph into a winter forest where spring flowers blossom in the background.

3 | The rods and cones that inform our visual awareness are transformed into spirals, circles, cylinders and helixes, creating a floral motif based on geometric forms.

4 | This motif references traditional chintz fabric but overlays it with floral sketches that give it a contemporary twist.

3   4

1   Russell clashes cultures and styles, depicting Samurai warriors and Indian swordsmen. The swordsman's sartorial details are intricately drawn by hand, as is the pixellated font included in the motif.

2   Boldly drawn in black and white lines, this abstract piece features lush tropical foliage.

3   Russell's painterly approach merges the exotic and the everyday, accentuated by pairing soft pastel shades and bold primary colours.

2

3

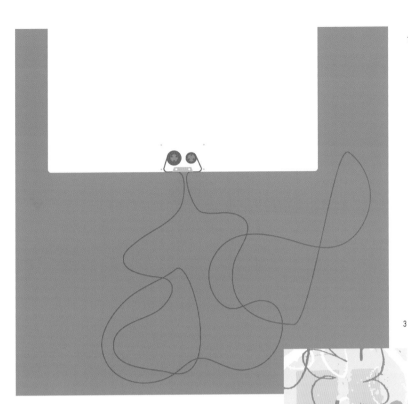

1&4   By combining a variety of references, ranging from bold graffiti tagging to simple line drawing, Russell creates a uniquely street motif. The repeated diagonal lines give the pattern a striped effect.

2   Typography, organic forms and anamorphic shapes are super-imposed against a hand-drawn grid in this colourful design.

3   Russell makes use of a single, meandering line traced into a figurative abstraction, which acts as a bridge between positive and negative spaces.

5   In this print, classic flower designs are foiled through the use of repeated lines and loosely-sketched outlines of flowers.

3

5

4

ANGEL CHANG

The manifesto of fashion's future may have been written by Angel Chang, the New York-based designer whose meteoric rise to fame was sparked by her techno-savvy prints and interactive clothing. At a time when most American designers buy pattern fabrics by the metre or source licenced prints from an agency, Chang's work is rooted in highly individual motifs that 'mean something. Making my own prints gives the collections deeper layers of meaning, which makes the garment as interesting to wear as it was to design,' she says.

Even before Chang left her hometown in Indiana to study in New York, the dream to launch her own label had already taken hold. She finished her art studies, interned at Viktor & Rolf and accepted a job at Donna Karan, where she was responsible for the fabric embroidery and print designs. Launching her own label in spring 2007, she explored the potentials of 'smart' fabrics and collaborated with engineers and interactive designers to develop new ways of dressing the urban woman. The collection included a nylon raincoat hand-embroidered with conductive wires that lit up. Pieces from the collection were featured in *The New York Times*, *Newsweek*, style.com and *Elle*, and at the end of the season she was awarded the prestigious 2007 Ecco Domani Fashion Foundation award for womenswear.

Chang says that, for her, technology is a natural choice: 'My generation of women is so different from previous ones. We work harder, travel more, manage all aspects of our lives through hand-held organizers, mobile phones and the Internet. Doesn't it seem odd to you that in recent decades women's lifestyles have moved forward so dramatically yet their clothing has not?' When Chang talks about the integration of clothing and technology, she advocates a seamless merger of the two. 'Technology can easily be concealed within the design, like it is in my metallic-finished knit hoodie with iPod controls. Or my Edwardian-inspired jacket, also made from conductive textiles, which functions as an MP3 player. I love embroidery, so it was a natural choice for me to hand-embroider buttons on the sleeve that cue the MP3 player to play, stop, fast forward and rewind, and control volume.'

Once Chang has financial backing in place she plans to incorporate wireless technology into most of her designs. 'My interest in technological innovation is strong, and so

1 | Angel Chang cuts and layers fabrics to create textured surfaces that move with the body. This tiered dress from her Spring/Summer 2008 collection is printed with the Red Maps Manhattan print.

3

2

4

2&4 | Inspired by motifs from old kimono fabrics, these prints have a distinctive Japanese feel. The dragon, engulfed by yellow flames, is mirrored for a symmetrical effect, also a feature of the blue pattern. Both are printed in thermochromatic dyes that change colour when exposed to the wearer's body heat.

3 | This blouse is made in Chang's semi-transparent, skin-toned silk jacquard 'nude' fabric.

is my desire to adapt fabric to provide the technological solutions that women need,' Chang says. 'Until I have the backing to do that, I'm aligning with technology little by little, beginning with my prints. That's why the thermochromatic dyes and UV-activated motifs feature so strongly in my work. They're affordable and fun, and a springboard to bigger ideas.'

Chang's heat-sensitive camouflage repeat is printed with thermochromatic dye. Printed on a pleated raglan sleeve dress and a georgette tunic, it makes the garments more see-through when it disappears. 'That collection includes some fun prints,' Chang says. 'Like the white-on-white "invisible" grid motif that I printed on chiffon. The pattern only becomes visible when exposed to UV light.'

Chang's Spring/Summer 2008 collection was inspired by the female secret agents of World War II chronicled in books such as *Women Who Lived for Danger* (Marcus Binney) and *Sisterhood of Spies* (Elizabeth McIntosh). Chang took a trip to the Spy Museum in Washington, DC, and returned to New York feeling inspired to draw motifs based on hidden maps, fighter planes and encrypted messages. 'A technician helped me transform my drawings of tanks, rifles and fighter jets into optical illusion stereogram images,' Chang explains. 'I printed them along the borders of A-line skirts, where they looked like ordinary abstract prints. Once you focus on them and soften your gaze, the stereogram image leaps out at you.'

One of Chang's signature prints is a Manhattan map motif that she developed in conjunction with Red Maps, who publish upmarket urban guides. The heat-sensitive dye used to print the motif only becomes legible when exposed to warmth, otherwise the fabric appears to be completely opaque. Another heat-sensitive motif was transferred onto pleated georgette. 'The thermochromatic dye can react to body heat, sunlight and ambient heat, and as it intensifies the prints fade into a soft glow,' Chang explains. 'I tease my clients that they have to be careful not to embarrass themselves, because their dresses may blush even if they don't.'

1   By rotating a classic geometrical grid 90 degrees, Chang create a motif with a diamond pattern.

2   This embroidered dress from her Spring/Summer 2008 collection was inspired by a drive through the French countryside. Chang sent sketches from her journey to craftspeople in India who embroidered the impressions onto the dresses by hand.

1

3 ┊ This silk jacquard chiffon blouse
┊ from the Spring/Summer 2008
┊ collection is embellished with a
┊ gold spider web lace motif.

4 ┊ Chang often relies on minimal
┊ details to create maximum effect,
┊ as in this simple knot.

5 ┊ This silk georgette blouse is
┊ ornamented with fluorescent
┊ organza panels.

5

3

4

1

3

2

4

1& Chang's Red Maps Manhattan print is
3-4 featured in this Whisper Tiered Ruffle
Top from her Spring/Summer 2008
collection. The print also features in
the scarf, shown with a racer back
tank top and crocheted by hand.

2 A close-up of her embroidered fabric
shown previously (page 22). Although
it was inspired by the tranquil
countryside of southern France,
the motif is named Battlefield.

6

5

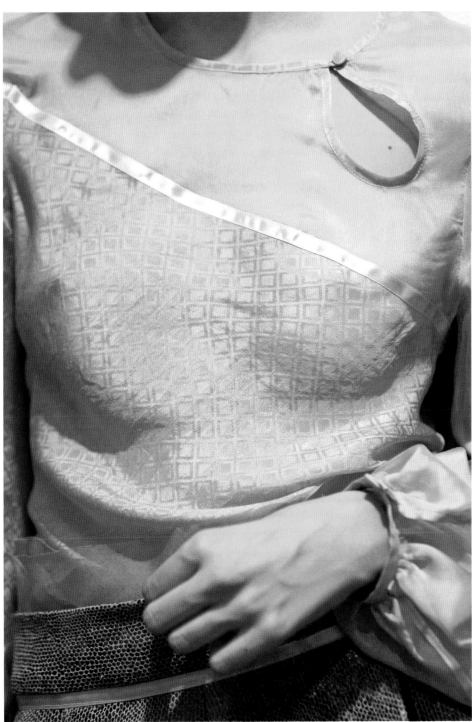

5-6 | Chang's 'nude' silk jacquard fabric
surface is printed with a subtle
geometric motif designed to make
the garment more opaque.

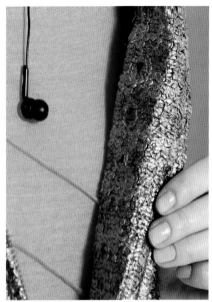

1-2 This print, shown previously (page 24), uses inks that change colour immediately in hot weather, or more gradually as it senses the wearer's body heat. Here, the motif is shown on a pleated chiffon tunic dress.

3-4 Chang decided to trim her pleated satin mini dress in fur in order to experiment with permanent fragrance. These fur cuffs are permeated with plant essences that retain their scent even after they are laundered.

5-6 This sportswear hoodie was knitted from metallic fibres capable of conducting digital signals. The garment is made with integrated iPod controls that fuse textiles and technology in a single expression.

ANITA
AHUJA

Around 6,000 cubic tonnes of waste hit the streets of Delhi every day. Most of it ends up in huge, reeking piles, and if Delhi's residents didn't take recycling into their own hands, the situation would probably get a lot worse.

Thanks to Anita Ahuja, whose pioneering work transforms trash into trendy textiles, beauty can still be found in the midst of so much rubbish. The non-profit organization Ahuja established in 1998 is aptly named Conserve, and comprises teams of people who reclaim the polyethylene bags dumped on the street and deliver them to her workshop, where they are sorted, washed and subsequently compressed by heat in an oven-like apparatus. Together with a team of traditional tailors, Ahuja and her staff cut and sew the non-woven fabrics they create, producing fashion accessories such as handbags, evening bags, beach bags, totes, shoppers, belts, footwear and jewellery.

It would be easy to mistake Conserve for a fashion label or a brand of sustainable textiles, but the products themselves are only a by-product of what Ahuja set out to do. 'My starting point wasn't so much ridding Delhi's streets of its garbage, but to help the rag-pickers, a community of people who are the weakest and the poorest, literally the outcasts of Indian society.' The caste of people assigned the title of 'rag-pickers' was formed several thousand years ago. They live solely on what others throw away, and are often marginalized within Indian society. Many of them have limited access to education and health benefits, but the people in Ahuja's employ are able to send their children to school and maintain a stable household.

Although Conserve enables the workers to improve their circumstances immediately, Ahuja is also focused on achieving long-term goals. 'Conserve contributes to a development of a new consciousness for the rag-pickers, which enables them to progressively become aware of their value as they have opportunities to become more prosperous individually and as a community,' Ahuja explains. 'Conserve is not limited to clothing the body or creating stylish products. We want our fabric to be beautiful and amazing in a way that empowers the mind and elevates the spirit.'

Ahuja believes that fabric is the ideal medium for uplifting Conserve's artisans and consumers. 'Textiles are based on the fundamental human values of love, integrity and joy. Hand-spun Indian textiles were once loaded with emotion, but today, because of industrialization, there is an emotional hollowness towards them. We need to stir passions about textiles, and recycled fabrics do that.'

Ahuja regards her unique take on textiles to be more closely aligned with global issues such as urban ecology and sustainable growth than with the textile industry. 'Conserve is not a part of a contemporary textile movement, I feel it is the beginning of something bigger,' she says. 'But beginnings are always small. You go to Gangotri where the Ganges River begins and you see a few drops trickling. And one cannot believe that these trickling drops are going to create the Ganges, but they do.'

1-2 | Anita Ahuja's non-woven fabrics
&4 | are made through a special heat process that fuses recycled plastics together. As different colours are overlaid and bonded together, unique varieties of striped textiles are created. Because each textile length is made from different colour combinations, no two fabrics are ever the same.

3 | The fabrics are made into stylish fashion accessories, as seen in this chic handbag made from her Brick Lane fabric trimmed with faux leather.

5 | Recycled paper can also be bonded with the plastic textile, as shown in this shopping bag.

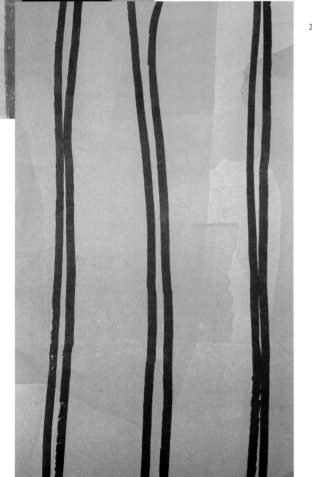

4

3

2

5

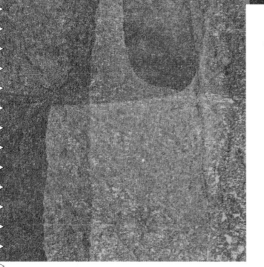

1

4

2

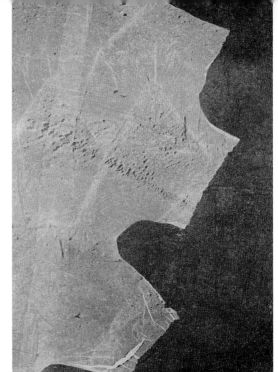

1–5 The discarded polyethylene bags, regarded as an eyesore in many urban areas, provided both the inspiration and the material for Conserve's recycled non-woven textiles. The textiles are sorted by colour and combined to make monochromatic tones such as Cosmos (1) and Red Wine (4), or clashed to create motifs such as Brick Lane (2), Golden Night (3) and Beach (5).

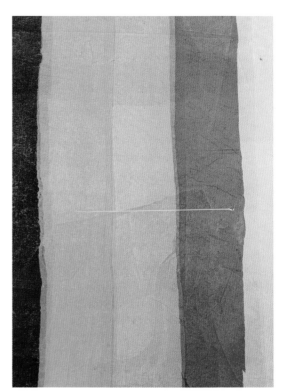

3

5

6

8

Ahuja's tote bags are a universal design that are popular in many different countries. Their outer shells are crafted from her non-woven fabric and lined with polyester inside.

6

Her Dick L make-up bag is made in her Brick Lane fabric. It is lined with polyester and trimmed in faux leather.

7

The Eucalyptus fabric is created by fusing layers of light blue and light green polythene together.

8

The Cricket fabric is a popular design for bags and accessories.

9

7

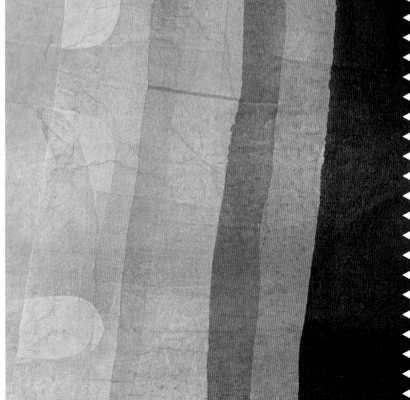

9

BECKY EARLEY

London-based designer Becky Earley is not as famous as she ought to be. A pioneering practitioner who charts the boundaries of new fabrics and forges fresh directions for old fibres, Earley's contribution to British textiles is really something.

Right now, Earley is lauded for her commitment to sustainable textiles. She is widely known as one of the first designers to print onto light-absorbing fleece made from recycled plastic bottles, and for breaking fresh ground by developing eco-friendly printing processes as well as coming up with a new paradigm of garment recycling. But before that, while still a student at Central St Martin's College of Art & Design in London, Earley decided to buck the norm of designing floral prints, feminine repeats and bold colour-ways. She skived off to the photography department one day and developed a 'heat photogram' method while she was down there. She gathered real items such as pins, steel mesh, aluminium foil, barbed wire and gritty scavenged finds she had picked up on the street, then applied her process to these to create permanent prints on cloth. The prints that resulted were striking in their lucidity. Since then, photographs have loomed large in her work.

It's no surprise, then, that Earley's friends like to tease her by claiming that she is probably one of the most widely-published photographers in Britain. Her heat photogram images are printed onto textiles rather than photographic paper, but they have been reproduced by the thousands. Earley's photographs have adorned countless magazine covers, and have rocketed to paparazzi fame when worn by celebrities such as Björk, Kylie Minogue and Zoë Ball. Earley shrugs it all off, saying it's probably because of her dad. 'He bought me a camera when I was ten, and all I wanted to do for years was take pictures,' she says. 'Maybe it was a surprise that I chose textiles instead of photography, but when I started printing my pictures on fabric, everyone knew where it came from.'

There is much more to Earley's work than pictures; her imagery provides imaginary keys that unlock a gateway into several real worlds. Although her prints are sometimes described as realism, to her they are anything but. 'Don't they bring an element of surrealism to textile design? I've taken photographs of models' hands and feet and printed them onto garments – really edgy stuff that artists like

1 Becky Earley was one of the first
textile designers to experiment
with recycled materials, low
impact printing processes and
PET-based fabrics. Her motifs
often feature floral abstractions.

Björk loved. Some of my favourite photos were the ones of tatty garments that I had found somewhere, which I airbrushed, coloured and photoshopped to make them beautiful. Transforming a rag into a glamourous textile isn't realism – it's the opposite.'

The b.earley label was launched in 1994, assisted by funding from the British Crafts Council and the Prince's Trust. From a tiny studio in London's Brick Lane, b.earley launched substantial production runs. 'I guess by 1998–99 we must have averaged 800 hand-printed scarves per week,' Earley says, 'which were distributed to 26 stockists worldwide.' Earley was hands-on in the production process, which quickly showed her how toxic textile production could be. 'Everything was filthy all the time. It was uncomfortable for the people working there, and damaging to the environment. At one point in 1999 I looked around and thought "What can I clean up here?" and so I started developing my "exhaust printing" process.' Like exhaust dyeing, exhaust printing reuses the original dye solution for every garment in the production run. It recycles the chemicals, minimizing water pollution and chemical waste. 'None of my clients wanted to buy a whole production run at first because the image fades in the process and gives each garment a unique colour-way,' Earley says. 'To me, that was a major selling point, because the production run created a group of unique items to sell rather than just a series of multiples.'

Earley has decided to address the growing problem of post-consumer waste, coming up with a method of recycling the millions of garments that are worn for one season and cast off when trends move forward. 'From working in the industry, I knew that Marks & Spencer have researched micro-fibre polyester and produce blouses that are long-lasting,' Earley explains. 'But I also knew that they dated quickly and end up in the rubbish. So I order them from textile recycling plants outside London, where I buy them by the bale. They're almost always in perfect condition, occasionally there'll be a balsamic vinegar stain or something, which doesn't make any difference because I over-print them anyway. Many of them are also re-cut by sonic slitting that reconfigures the seams or incorporates a few new design details.'

Earley currently holds the coveted research position of Reader Fellow at Chelsea College of Art & Design in London, but continues to develop her own label. 'I teach and co-ordinate research projects in the college and outside it,' Earley says. 'When I'm there

I'm analyzing how other design disciplines are finding ways to become more environmentally friendly and seeing what textile designers can learn from them.' Earley's research will be published in a book which proposes seven strategies for eco-friendly textile design, due be released in 2009. 'When I'm not at the college you'll probably find me in the wooden eco lodge at the bottom of my garden, sitting behind my computer. It's a great place to think. I think a lot about the future of textile design and I want to develop new strategies to minimize the amount of waste.'

Earley's unique oeuvre positions her between several worlds: the creative forum of her studio practice, the analytical industry 'watchdog' and the theoretical realm of academia. But which one does she really belong to? 'I've got my fingers in several pies right now,' Earley says. 'I love having a small studio and my own label and I also love what I do at the college. I think what I love most is feeling that I belong to a whole new breed of textile designers, who are thinking, theorizing and researching just as much as they are dreaming, imagining and creating. Professionals that can use their knowledge of textiles and systems and design whole new environments. To me that's exciting, because that's what the future needs.'

1

2

1-4 The designs Earley exhibited at the 'Ever and Again' eco-fashion exhibition in 2008 demonstrated how added value could be given to discarded fabric forms so that they could be worn again. Earley outlines a new paradigm for prolonging the lifespan of clothing by reconfiguring them, dying them and embellishing them with embroidery and appliqué.

3

4

1–2 Earley's pioneering printing techniques result in motifs that are edgy and elegant. Trompe l'oeil imagery creates pleated effects that give the fabrics another dimension.

3 This dramatic black and white motif was created for Earley's Top 100 project, an initiative to salvage discarded tops and remake them in themed sets of ten. She refers to the project as 'upcycling' rather than 'recycling' because the spectacular garments that result are much more interesting than they were in their original forms.

3

1

1-4 Earley's Worn Again project takes upcycling further by finding new technologies that will create new possibilities for textile recycling. Exhaust printing processes and new dying techniques enable her to minimize post-consumer waste by giving old garments new life. As she combines creativity and ecological ethics in fabric form, her work renders a new understanding of what the ecological goals of diversity, participation, efficiency and zero waste can mean for fashion textiles.

3

2

4

C.NEEON

Imagine a place where booze is cheap and rents cost next to nothing, where everyone sleeps through breakfast and rolls out of bed at lunchtime, where the party never ends and traditional office jobs seem like a thing of the past. And all the locals are cool, creative and beautiful.

Look no further than East Berlin, a heady hotspot where the lofty industrial spaces of the former communist block are inhabited by artists, filmmakers, photographers and designers. Trendy textiles also factor in the mix, because this is where the design duo of Clara Leskovar and Doreen Schulz, also known as c.neeon, have set up shop. 'We work in a house with a big garden shared with a lot of other designers and artists,' Leskovar says. 'You wanted to know what drives us? Well, this is it. The exchange between all these creative people is our biggest source of inspiration.'

c.neeon was formed when textile designer Clara (who is the 'c' part of c.neeon) and fashion designer Doreen (nicknamed 'Neeon' when she was small) decided to fuse their print design and cutting skills and launch a fashion label. 'It's the combination of skills that produces the c.neeon look,' Leskovar says. 'Pattern cutting does not play the main role in our work, it is equal to the print design. A lot of people think that we make asymmetric cuts, but that's not what we do at all. I guess the colours we use and the abstract motifs can create an impression of asymmetry.'

Berlin is often compared to New York in the 1980s, and perhaps that was why the British press once stated that many of the colours and shapes that characterized the decade find expression in c.neeon's prints. 'Actually, not at all,' Leskovar says. 'The print inspirations actually go back much further than the 80s. One winter collection was inspired by the Russian artist Tamara Lempicka, and other collections have been influenced by the Vienna Werkstätte and Russian Constructivism. That said, modern art is not our only inspiration.'

When c.neeon start working on a new collection, they seem to operate as a single entity capable of carrying out individual tasks in tandem. Leskovar describes c.neeon's design process as a creative free-for-all, where 'in the beginning of a new collection each is collecting for herself, bringing in the things that make her curious or inspired, like music, books or just small things in everyday life. We

1&3   The inspiration behind c.neeon's Autumn/Winter 2007 collection was a cult song from the East German band 'keks'. The song's original lyrics were considered to be so controversial that they were almost entirely censored, and only the refrain 'hasch mich mädchen' (catch me girl) remained. The simple beat and the repetition of the three words had such strong resonance with the design duo that the resulting collection was named 'haschmichmädchen'.

2   This print, from the Love You Delicious collection, reveals how their graphic approach results in fabric motifs that move easily between garments, fashion accessories and interior textiles.

2

3

usually see that we have collected items which are quite similar. Then the next step is to make some collages, which create a certain atmosphere and give an impression of the proportions for the next collection.' At that point Leskovar starts concentrating on the motifs, while Schulz starts cutting the patterns for the next collection. Neither considers their work to be complete until the other is satisfied with her own designs. 'It's very important for us that we do not hold on to a certain impression of the collection in our minds until we both have finished what we're doing.'

Although the fusion of pattern cutting and print design has historical precedents, c.neeon may have reclaimed it as a new model for twenty-first-century fashion. 'Throughout fashion history, textile design was always important. There were always examples of designers who emphasized cutting, but there were others who preferred print design just as much. For Doreen and I, both subjects have endless facets, and these different possibilities will always be fascinating for us.'

2

1&
3-4

Shown in London in 2005,
c.neeon's collection, entitled Do
you remember the first time?, was
inspired by the Pulp song of the
same name. The designers captured
the beat on fabric by representing
the rhythm in repeating lines.

3

4

2 Entitled Sharing Secrets, c.neeon's
Autumn/Winter 2008 collection
reflected their interest in the artist
Tamara Lempicka, who, although
known for her paintings, also
produced graphics for sportswear.
The collection's colour palette was
based on those found in Tamara
Lempicka's paintings, and the
geometric motifs and fragmented
shapes were based on the artist's
signature style.

1-4 These garments, from the Do you remember the first time? collection shown previously (see page 42), feature vibrant motifs that represent movement and speed. The simple, unstructured cuts of the collection bring sportswear to mind, recalling the comfortable, free-flowing silhouettes worn by yoga enthusiasts and martial arts practitioners. Shorts and hoods underlined the collection's sporty mood, while bold colours and racy stripes embellish the garments with a dynamic surface.

1

2

4

3

2

1–2 Designed for the Sharing Secrets collection, the motifs for these garments are evocative of the Art Deco style that inspired them. The patterns are drawn with precision, interspersing blocks of solid colour with bold geometric repeats.

3   c.neeon set a new standard for hooded jersey tops when they designed this one for the 'haschmichmädchen' collection. The jersey's traditional drawstring whipcord has been replaced with braided cords that run through the hood and cross over the chest as they fasten in each shoulder.

4   The fractal pattern printed on the fabric of these trousers is echoed in their angular cut and unconventional fit.

1–4 More garments from Love You Delicious (page 41), c.neeon's Spring/Summer 2008 collection, featuring prints inspired by a piece of candy bought in Shanghai. 'I bought an entire bag, flattened the wrappers carefully, flew around half the globe and spread the 30 pieces over my kitchen table in Berlin,' Leskovar recalls. 'It said "love you delicious" on each one of them.' The garments that resulted were crafted in transparent, layered fabrics such as silk voile and chiffon, and constructed in silhouettes inspired by the shapes created by the overlaid candy wrappers.

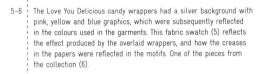

5-6 | The Love You Delicious candy wrappers had a silver background with pink, yellow and blue graphics, which were subsequently reflected in the colours used in the garments. This fabric swatch (5) reflects the effect produced by the overlaid wrappers, and how the creases in the papers were reflected in the motifs. One of the pieces from the collection (6).

6

1 : Designed for the Local Foreigner
    Spring/Summer 2007 collection, this
    motif was printed on to a square of
    fabric, slit across the centre, and
    folded over the torso to create the
    upper part of a high-waisted dress.

2-4 : The same collection intends to
    challenge familiar and foreign
    influences. It is based on a
    soundtrack from Berlin band
    Planningtorock, where lead singer
    Janine Rostron, a British-born
    resident of Berlin, describes the city
    in the eyes of a 'local foreigner'. The
    garments are cut closer to the body
    than in previous collections, and
    features fine knits and diaphanous
    cottons that give the garments a
    distinctively feminine feel.

1

3

2

4

5 | The prints in the Local Foreigner collection were based on vertically or diagonally mirrored triangles interspersed with fine lines and which contrast bold, monochromatic fields. Some of the patterns mimic the folds of origami, capturing them on a two-dimensional colour field.

5

CARLENE EDWARDS

Carlene Edwards is based in Italy, but her work transcends virtually all borders. Born in London and educated in Scotland, today Edwards works full-time for Italian manufacturer Friulprint, who export her textile designs worldwide. Edwards is acclaimed for her fusion of two-dimensional design techniques; most of her designs are drawn by hand or created through mixed media, and some include motifs created in CAD.

The sleepy town of Tarcento, where Friulprint is based, is rather subdued in comparison to Hackney, the inner-city London borough where Edwards grew up. Urban life has been Edwards' biggest source of inspiration so far, resulting in collections such as Inner City Living and Hip Hopular. 'I like my work to tell a story,' Edwards says. 'For one collection, I studied the pages of the *Hackney Gazette*, which was my local newspaper at the time, to find articles about children's projects, artistic performances, musical events and cultural festivals. It wasn't easy to spot them immediately, because they were eclipsed by the headline articles about violence and crime that dominated the newspaper. I realized that inner city areas even get bad press locally, with little media attention given to the wealth of creativity that exists in the community.'

Edwards decided to capture all aspects of local life in her prints. 'Not just my own experience, but the things that make up the background of so many people's daily routines,' she says. 'I wanted to create prints that reflect how we live, our surroundings and environments.' Her Inner City Living collection evolved from sketches of the area and personal photographs taken around the borough of Hackney. The prints are poetic portrayals of the derelict buildings, fencing, scaffolding and graffiti-covered brick walls that characterize parts of Hackney, but also capture the neighbourhood's artistic and cultural identity. 'The Hip Hopular series was inspired by young Hackney. Hip Hop culture, parties, style, fashion and attitude all fed into the designs.'

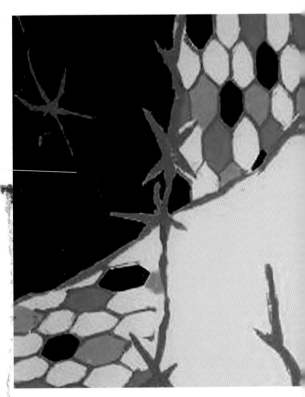

The gritty edges of Edward's urban decay imagery are often softened by pattern repeats and contrasting colour-ways. 'My colour schemes are deliberately vibrant and positive,' Edwards says, 'to reflect the fashion sensibilities of most inner-city communities. Colours and motifs from sportswear, high street fashion and African textiles have been a source of inspiration for me. I mix these elements with my drawings and photography, and other elements of youth culture such as Hip Hop music. That's where motifs such as trainers, shoelaces and headphones come from.'

Her acute insight into street fashion has enabled Edwards to identify shortcomings that she hopes textile designers can make up for. 'There aren't enough cool prints for women's streetwear,' Edwards laments. 'Here we are, left with florals again. Not that I don't like flowers, but I'd like to see more edgy designs. Men's streetwear prints are much more diverse. Some fashion labels are starting to use interesting womenswear prints, so hopefully that will continue.'

Edwards points out that edgy fabric prints aren't just a part of urban life, or merely a passing trend. 'Textiles are everywhere and part of our everyday lives – in our homes, at work, our uniforms, our fashion. What we wear is a big part of how we express ourselves. I love fashion and get a buzz from creating designs that people choose to wear.'

2

3

4

STANd UP

stANd UP

1 | Carlene Edwards fuses a variety of two-dimensional design techniques in her work. Many of her designs are sketched by hand or painted, and some of her motifs are created in CAD.

2 | Urban life is a big source of inspiration for some of her collections. This motif, entitled Fenced In, evokes the barbed wire barriers and chain-link fences that close off no-go zones within the inner city.

3 | Noticing that there were too few edgy prints made for women's streetwear, Edwards designed some of her own, such as the Brickwall pattern, from which she produced this scarf.

4 | Rebellious sentiments often feature in the designer's work, whether expressed subtletly in a motif or voiced more loudly through the use of text, as shown in this print.

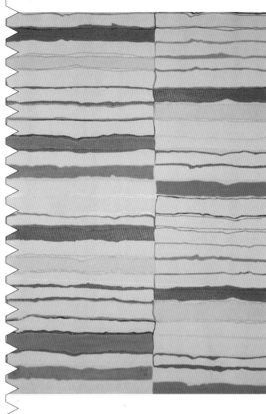

1

1   Edwards takes a painterly approach
to print design, creating horizontal
stripes that appear more like
brushstrokes on canvas than motifs
printed on fabric.

2&4   This simple print is eye-catching
and vibrant, whether printed as
a single or repeated pattern.

3&6   Designed in 2005, the Headphones
motif is one of Edwards' most
popular patterns. She has produced
several versions of it for a range
of garments and accessories.

5   Her work is characterized by vivid
colours that are often based on
themes and patterns discovered
in urban settings.

7   This print takes its inspiration
from the geometric patterns
of brickwork, transformed by
Edwards into abstract designs.

3

4

2

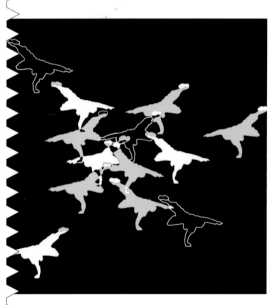

5

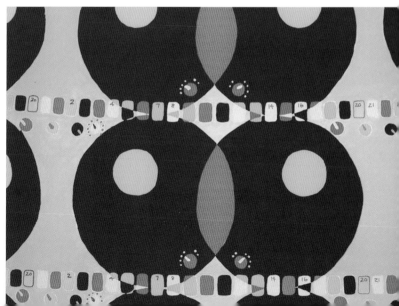

6

7

Hip Hop music and dance clubs are 1
also references for Edwards' work.

One of the designer's cityscape 2
prints. Evolving from sketches
made in an urban area,
she transforms graffiti, derelict
buildings and abandoned bicycles
into striking designs.

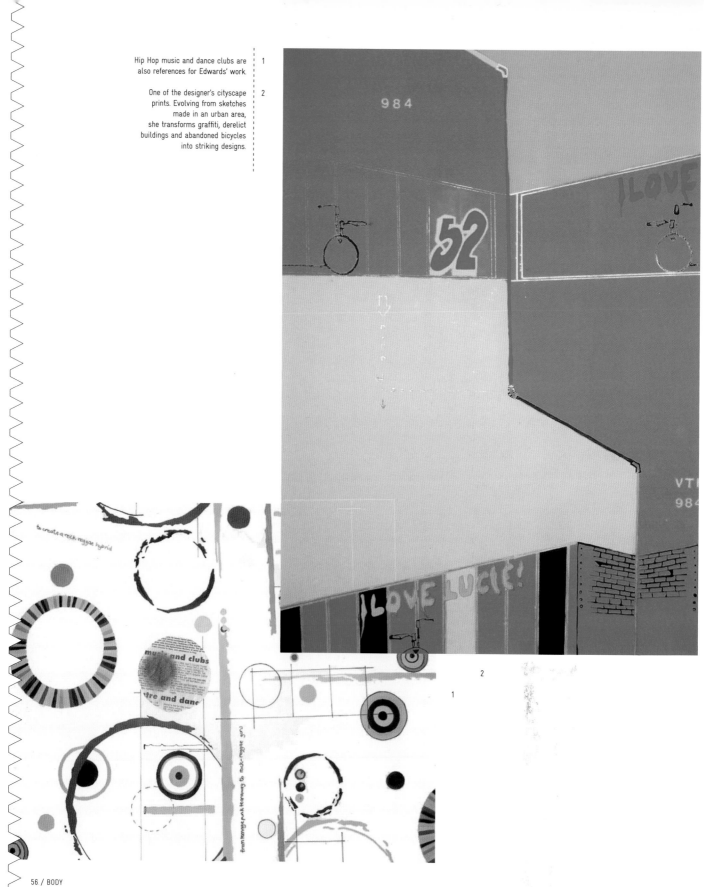

2

1

3 Enitled Laces 2, the circular shapes in this design are created from shoelaces.

4 In this motif, Edwards identifies the supermarket trolley, often found abandoned in the streets of a city, as a universal icon of our times.

5 Grids, grates and fences offer an endless source of geometric shapes for the designer.

3

4

5

CLARE TOUGH

Affectionately described as 'Tough by name and tough by nature', British designer Clare Tough has what it takes to succeed in the fashion industry. Tough rose to knitwear fame even before she completed her MA degree at Central St Martin's College of Art & Design in London. Her graduate collection was described by *Vogue* as 'the future of British fashion', and was immediately snapped up by British retailers.

Tough is considered to be a visionary in constructed textiles. Her collections are characterized by the juxtapositions of oversized, extravagant shapes and streamlined, body-hugging silhouettes embellished with clever details. Metallic contours are typically stitched around the bust line, while horizontal panels are drawn together to create corseted effects. 'I think the idea behind my work is to find a way of using traditional techniques in a modern context,' Tough says. 'I like designing distinctive silhouettes and that's usually where I begin. Layering is also something that I like to create. I start with tight things underneath and contrast them with bigger shapes that I build layer by layer.'

Her collections often incorporate rigid materials that initially seem incongruous to the delicate yarns she uses. 'For me, knitwear gets interesting when you find something unusual in it,' Tough says. 'The contrast of a soft structure and a piece of metal is unexpected, so it's fun to wear. Hard materials add more structure to a knitwear design, and sometimes that's what enables me to come up with interesting shapes.'

Tough uses various knitting techniques to integrate metal with yarn; she has found a way to fuse knitted yarns with silver wire, and uses both hand- and machine-knit techniques to combine metal chain with yarn. 'There are many different combinations of materials and techniques I could experiment with,' Tough says. 'For example, lambswool is a great fibre to use with metal. From time to time I combine it with a found object I want to add to a garment, and I've used it to crochet key rings together.'

Teaming up with the Istanbul-based label Black Dot in Spring/Summer 2008, Tough launched a collaboration described as her second line. The collection fused traditional Turkish craft techniques with state-of-the-art knitting technology. Tough created oversized silhouettes based on the billowing shapes of Ottoman trousers and cropped harem pants, which she paired with slinky tunics and jersey tops, and layered with hooded tops, snug cardigans and casual waistcoats. Tough's signature material was represented in Lurex® threads interwoven with cashmere or with linen yarns blended with silk fibres.

Tough believes that her success may reflect a growing appreciation of knitwear worldwide. 'Knitwear is becoming more and more popular every year,' she says. 'It's definitely on the up. For many years knitwear was considered to be a lesser part of the collection, but now it plays a bigger role in the main collections. And knitwear is worn year-round today – you see it in Spring/Summer collections more now than ever before.' As the increased popularity of knitwear sparks a growing demand for her work, Tough is quickly becoming recognized as a leading force in the industry. When it comes to knitwear, it certainly is Tough at the top.

1 Clare Tough's Spring/Summer 2008 collection was characterized
by twisted yarns, scalloped effects, double-sided weft and warp
knits, and vibrant motifs. This one-piece swimsuit and hat are
simply embellished with metal details, while this zipped cardigan
is adorned with colourful zig-zags.

2 The vivid motifs adorning this
short-sleeved dress transform
the wearer into a walking mural,
elevating traditional knitwear to
new heights.

3 Intricate embroidery is juxtaposed
against a background of muted
greys and blacks in this hooded
top and mini dress.

2

3

Tough's work is often described as   1–3
'urban knitwear', and these designs
from her Spring/Summer 2008
collection literally brought the
cityscape to life. The shoulder bag
is embroidered with the Manhattan
skyline, interpreting architectural
shapes as tactile motifs (1).

Tough's bikini top recreates the   4
Manhattan Bridge and surrounding
DUMBO neighbourhood, while the
bikini bottoms afford a truly unique
panorama of the Statue of Liberty.

4

3

2

1

1–3 | The MA graduate show Tough presented at London Fashion Week in 2004 showcased a new vision for knitwear. The designs fused several different techniques and different types of yarns to create richly textured rings and net-like panels. The collection received rave reviews in the British press, and was bought up by leading British retailers.

4-5 | The asymmetry of the patterns in the same MA graduate show was reflected in the garment's shapes, which featured wing-like sleeves and off-the-shoulder designs.

4

5

1

2

3

1-6 Tough's Autumn/Winter 2006
collection was a benchmark in
her work. It combined various
knitting techniques (hand, crochet,
machine, etc) with a surprising
range of materials. She developed
a method of knitting chain within
yarn, and embellished oversized
jumpers, mini dresses and tight
vests with lengths of gold- and
silver-coloured chains. She stitched
the chains into circular shapes
around the bust cut-away panels
on the sides to create these daring
knitwear designs.

5

4

6

3

4

5

1-5 The Spring/Summer 2007 collection featured loose fitting casual
designs with figure-hugging dresses that oozed sex appeal. Simple,
monochromatic separates featured alongside garments sporting
bold stripes and richly textured surfaces. The garments were crafted
from Lurex® threads interwoven with cashmere or with linen yarns
blended with silk fibres.

CLAUDIA HILL

'I'm not good with words,' says Claudia Hill, when we meet at her Brooklyn studio, 'so I could never describe all the feelings I express through my designs. But what I can do is work as a kind of emotional architect who captures expression in clothing, so that they can function as a portable diary for the people who wear them. After all, I am sculpting clothing as a house for the body. To me, a textile's surface, with all its subtle details, resembles the inside, the internal.'

Flowing freely between self-expression and art-like objects comes easily to Hill, who trained to be a dancer. She left her native Germany to continue her dance studies in New York, where she discovered that she also had a talent for costume design. A chance meeting with Spanish designer Miguel Adrover resulted in a commission for some pieces that he sold in his shop, Horn, in New York. 'I was in this beautiful flow from dance to design,' Hill remembers, 'and one moment I was making my own clothes, the next I was making them for Miguel's shop, and suddenly I was also making them for some clients in Japan.'

Hill eschews traditional catwalk shows and presents her collections through performances, installations and presentations held at her boutique in Berlin. 'I never considered adapting to the traditional fashion formats,' Hill says, 'because my work is about the one-off and not things that can be mass-produced. I really enjoy designing the textiles I use, whether they are new fabrics or found materials. Structuring my textiles enables me to be playful, experimental and find a way to break boundaries. That would never be possible with conventional fabrics.'

Some of Hill's fabrics are scented with herbs to add an intangible experience to the garment. Others are weighted with stones sewn into tiny pouches created by rouching the fabric, enabling it to hang in a certain way or acquire a unique texture. Hill has even made her own lace, regarding the open structure of the lace to be the antithesis of the closed surface surrounding the stones. 'Lacemaking is an ancient craft,' Hill says, 'and making lace by hand today is the opposite of all the fast production cycles created by technology.'

Hill once famously shredded a man's suit, then knitted it into a cocktail dress. 'I loved the process of taking a man's garment and transforming it into something beautiful for

1

2

1-2 | To Claudia Hill, a garment's surface is a metaphor for feelings, thoughts and sentiments. She structures and sculpts her fabrics to make each garment a unique piece. Soft folds can create corsage-like detailing (1), while a collar (2) gives a garment a strong silhouette.

3-6 | Hill used to be a professional dancer and now uses clothing to explore the frontier between fashion and art, to explore the process of producing the garment more than the finished object. Here, a blouse is scrunched and hand-processed to give the fabric a wrinkled texture.

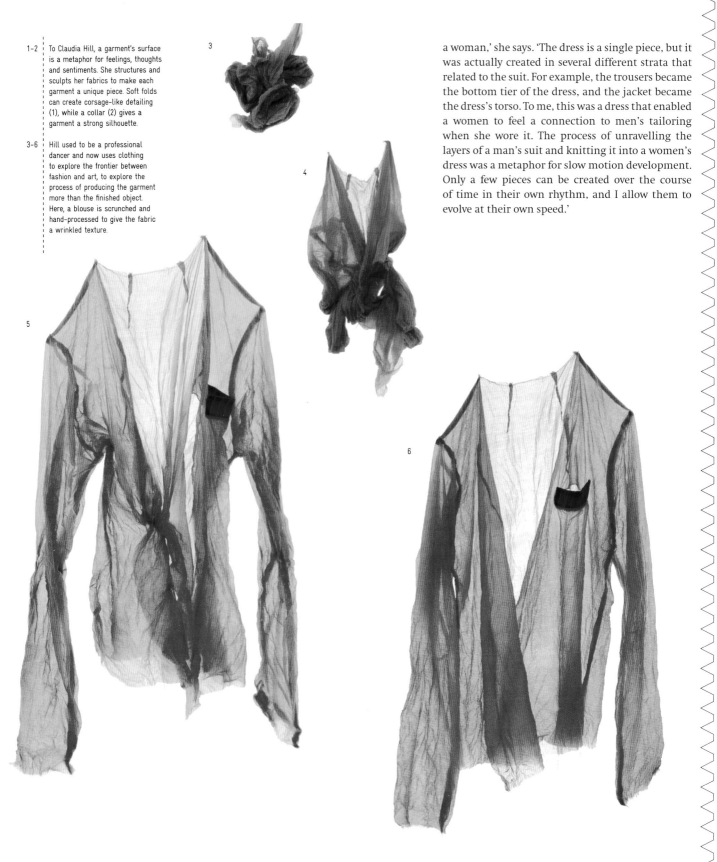

a woman,' she says. 'The dress is a single piece, but it was actually created in several different strata that related to the suit. For example, the trousers became the bottom tier of the dress, and the jacket became the dress's torso. To me, this was a dress that enabled a women to feel a connection to men's tailoring when she wore it. The process of unravelling the layers of a man's suit and knitting it into a women's dress was a metaphor for slow motion development. Only a few pieces can be created over the course of time in their own rhythm, and I allow them to evolve at their own speed.'

2

3

1   In Hill's creative hands, fabric remnants are a source of inspiration that provide her with raw material for one-off designs.

2   Hill often combines discarded fabrics with new materials, and sometimes incorporates small stones and dried herbs into the textile's structure.

3   Her knitwear is richly-textured and robust. This cardigan was knitted from salvaged materials.

4   The Autumn/Winter 2005 collection featured a man's suit, shredded and knitted into this dress. The trousers form the bottom tier of the dress, while the waistcoat and jacket were used for the torso.

5   Many of Hill's designs remain 'unfinished'. As it frays and unravels over time, it slowly morphs into a new form.

4

5

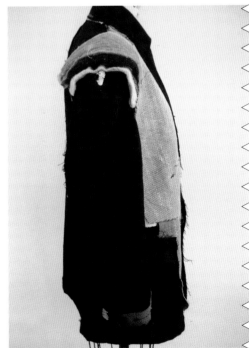

1   Hill makes her own lace, and she loves revitalizing and perpetuating a traditional craft form. To her, working in this way by hand is an important lo-tech skill that opposes the fast production cycles created by digital technology.

2   Stitching features are an important detail in these garments from the Spring/Summer 2006 collection. As they span the gap between two halves of the garment the threads form a gossamer panel. Zig-zagging across the side panels, they create an embroidered motif.

Although most of Hill's designs are edgy and ultra-modern, she sometimes celebrates the beauty of historic silhouettes. This jacket evokes the traditional kimono collar, which gives way to a ruffled Victorian shape.   3

The designer makes many of the garments by hand, taking her closer to couture practice than mainstream garment manufacture.   4

This knitted top and cape were produced from fabric scraps and discarded material.   5

3

4

5

FLORENCE MANLIK

At the stroke of a pen, Paris-based graphic artist Florence Manlik can move from art to fashion to design and back again. For her, a drawing is a space for thought, a place where she can freely express her ideas on paper first and live them out in another medium later. Manlik's work is unique in its synthesis of subject, structure and style, a quality that says as much about her art education as it does about her free-spirited nature. 'I consider myself to be an artist more than a designer, because I draw whatever I like,' Manlik says. 'Drawing is what roots me. It's what brings my ideas to the surface and allows them to exist. Textiles, along with other media, connects them to things, to people.'

Conscious that her work has many different applications, Manlik does not consider herself to be a textile designer per se, and describes the media she works in in terms of 'platforms' rather than products. 'There are many different platforms for the work I do,' she explains, 'because my drawings can easily adapt to many different surfaces. They may take shape as fashion prints on T-shirts, dresses, coats, hats and shoes, but they also adorn CD covers, record sleeves, book jackets, wallpaper and even the shop windows of Selfridges, where I was commissioned to design an ad campaign for the London store in autumn of 2007. They asked me to structure my drawings according to their brief, but most clients choose existing work.'

Many of Manlik's works are ethereal dreamscapes that draw the viewer into another world, and her fashion prints seem to provide an escape from the harsh realities of urban life as they are worn in the streets of Paris. Manlik descrbes Paris as an arena, where 'art is on the move, travelling through the city and accompanying people in everyday life – it's beautiful! We need that.'

Manlik never intended to specialize in fashion prints, but describes it as an aspect of her career that she enjoys a lot. Her graphic style has attracted commissions from Fenchurch, Parisian couturier Robert Normand and others such as Graniph in Japan, and Surface to Air. 'Fashion is a fantastic platform for me,' she says. I've always loved fashion and clothes, and I also love looking at well-dressed people. But when I saw Robert Normand's Autumn/Winter 2008 fashion show [where Manlik's textile designs were printed on almost every piece of the collection] I felt intense emotion. Printed garments are about making a show out of the body, and out of the clothes too. Fashion can be so spectacular, a true meeting of joy and desire.'

Robert Normand is an expressive designer who finds inspiration in art, architecture and graphic design, and usually incorporates a wide range of cultural references in his fashion collections. Normand typically catalogues his inspirations, systematically gathering books, images and materials as he works on the collection. 'He and I are very different in that respect,' Manlik says. 'He talks about how the collection will look and shows me images and objects that inspired him. I'm the opposite – I'm a true minimalist who only owns the essentials. I don't collect things or consciously store my inspirations in my imagination. Once I've grasped Robert's brief, he can let it go, and I make it mine. Then it feels like party time to me, and I start drawing and drawing.'

1–2   Florece Manlik first forayed into fashion when she collaborated with French designer Robert Normand. Her prints for his Spring/Summer 2008 catwalks were elegant and edgy.

Normand uses Manlik's patterns and motifs to add abstract, playful and surprisingly surrealistic touches to his designs, alternately hiding them in a small detail or blowing them up to large-scale proportions. 'Robert loves to imagine strange associations, especially mixing time periods together,' Manlik explains. 'The first time we worked together he came up with these crazy ideas of flying sharks drowning in a sea storm, with flower baskets woven out of hair... to me, visions like these feel so familiar that I didn't even notice it was someone else's fantasy.'

While fans of Manlik's work applaud the considered, almost obsessive precision that her work seems to convey, her own descriptions of her work reference it in terms of a 'spontaneous' and 'free-flowing' process. 'The way I draw is not predetermined, it's organic. A drawing grows and evolves, just branching out as if it was a plant. It sounds abstract to say that a drawing is a sum total of little coincidences, chances and lucky accidents, but the drawing comes together through lots of unexpected turns and details. I make them mine by recognizing the value of letting things evolve rather than by controlling every single detail. By the time it's finished, a drawing may end up stuffed with mushrooms and monsters, even though they may not have been the main inspiration. Their mission is to bring back some primal mystery and project it before our very eyes.'

As the interview draws to a close, Manlik's thoughts return to Normand. 'I felt uplifted by something I heard Robert say recently. He said, "Being a coquette is showing an appetite for life; it's the opposite of resignation".' That statement seems to sum up Manlik's work too: embracing life and showcasing the splendour of the human imagination, never giving in to the limitations of what the real world may normally expect.

2

1

1   Manlik's otherworldly aesthetic shows how unencumbered and expressive fashion motifs can be, creating a surface that lures the wearer into a world of dreamy enchantment.

2–3   Her black rose motif adds a note of Gothic elegance when applied to the silk garments.

4   Many of the prints Manlik designs for Robert Normand are developed in response to a specific garment, such as this motif that evokes the Far East.

5   Screen-printed onto pattern repeats, motifs merge traditional fabrics with cutting-edge surface design, to give classic cuts a contemporary update.

2

3

4

5

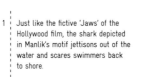

1   Just like the fictive 'Jaws' of the Hollywood film, the shark depicted in Manlik's motif jettisons out of the water and scares swimmers back to shore.

2   Whether expressed in bold prints or in the softly muted shown here, Manlik's prints seem closer to hand-painted artworks than typical textile prints.

3   Her work is far removed from the feminine motifs that most fashion designers prefer, and yet its soft shapes and subtle outlines complement the female form.

The wavy contours expressed in this motif suggest movement and texture, adding another dimension to this garment's sleek and streamlined silhouette.   4

Many designs are printed in a single colour, which gives them a powerful presence on the catwalk.   5

This close-up reveals how her three-dimensional approach to pattern design often results in oversized motifs that seek the language of fine art more than surface design.   6

FLORENCE MANLIK

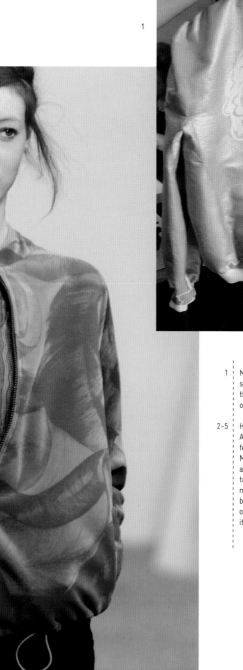

1

1 Manlik's elegant floral motifs, shown previously (page 76), give this classic bomber jacket an air of glamour.

2-5 Her designs for Robert Normand's Autumn/Winter 2008 collection are featured on almost every garment. Manlik's motifs add abstract, playful and surprisingly surrealistic touches to his designs. They are used in many guises; as a small detail, blown up to large-scale proportions, or 'hidden' inside the garment on its lining.

2

3

4

5

GUT'S DYNAMITE CABARETS

In Japanese, there are three words for clothing: *wafuku*, which means Japanese clothing; *yōfuku*, which means western clothing; and *fuku*, which means clothing in general. Apart from meaning clothes, *fuku* can also be used to describe good fortune or a feeling of happiness. When it comes to talking about their clothing, Gut's Dynamite Cabarets don't describe their collections as either *wafuku* or *yōfuku*. To them, what they do is pure *fuku*, because they take happiness as their starting point.

Before they launched their fashion label, Cabarets Aki and Jackal Kuzu had their own rock-n-roll band, which was also called Gut's Dynamite Cabarets. The band, which had been widely popular in Japan and still has a cult following today, gave them the perfect platform for cultivating their outrageous Rock Star style. Aki and Kuzu had studied fashion design at Bunka University in Tokyo before forming a band, so starting their own label seemed like a natural choice. The transition from songwriting to sartorial styling was easily made; they just shifted their trademark rock-n-roll cool from the music stage onto the fashion catwalk.

Today, Aki and Kuzu regard making music as important as designing garments and drawing prints, but labels such as 'musician', 'fashion designer' or 'textile designer' don't interest them anymore. They famously sum up their approach in a single statement: 'We're born crazy.' They were. Who else could stage a fashion show where both menswear and womenswear are modelled by men? Or cast the menswear models at a gay gym in Tokyo, choosing muscle boys to strut up and down the catwalk in between the sashaying strides of pouting, posing and hissing drag queens? Or play the catwalk soundtracks at top volume, because otherwise they'd get drowned out by the screaming of the audience? Most fashionistas will tell you that the norm at Tokyo fashion shows is for the audience to sit in polite silence and applaud quietly at the end of the show. But not here.

Gut's eclectic menswear and womenswear collections give Belgian wild child Walter Van Beirendonck a run for his money. Camp and over the top, their fashion shows are as in-your-face as those that once made John Galliano famous. An early fashion press review described one as 'a theatrical and eclectic ride taking in drag queens, macho boys and rock-n-roll that kept the fashion week audience

1   Animal prints, treated leather and faux fur set the tone for the Autumn/Winter 2007 collection, and Gut's Dynamite Cabarets designed their very own versions. Here, colourful Zebra-inspired fabric is paired with embossed leather and trimmed in faux fur.

2   The Autumn/Winter 2008 fashion collection showcased a lot of skin – faux animal prints as well as the models' bare flesh – to showcase Gut's new underwear line for that season.

suitably enthralled,' and the designers have lived up to this description ever since. 'We're just two straight guys who love gay culture. We love drag queens and blown-up, body-conscious sissy boys. The more camp it is and the more over-the-top and outrageous it is, the more we like it.'

The motifs that Aki and Kuzu design give their garments an edge that other labels don't have. They introduced a new dimension to the genre of animal prints with their witty renderings of copulating dogs, fornicating sheep and a menagerie of horny giraffes, rabbits and cats. Drawn in bold lines and coloured in fluorescent yellow, lime green, hot pink and electric blue, this print has a cartoon-like innocence that belies its sexual tone. Another motif plays with the idea of wearing 'the designer' – screen-printed cameo portraits are repeated on disco mini dresses, creating a wearable portrait gallery.

Aki and Kuzu describe scribbling as the basis for their motifs, often preferring naïve line drawings over elaborate patterns. Some prints border between robust graffiti tagging and cartoon-like, Pop Art drawings, while others have more in common with graphic design than they do with traditional textile prints. One of their most popular prints is a 'logo mania' design that depicts their logo in liquifying letters; as the typeface appears to dissolve, the effect is that of dripping wax streaming down the surface of the garment.

Whether or not Gut's Dynamite Cabarets are making western *yōfuku* or a new direction for Japanese *wafuku*, the term *fuku* will always describe their upbeat designs. Aki and Kuzu's happy prints bring a warming, feel-good factor to fashion that, judging by their screaming fans, will soon be heard all over the world.

1-3 | Gut's designs have a unique style.
They have introduced a new dimension
to the genre of fashion prints through
their autobiographical and animal
motifs with sexualized content.
The prints are sketched in bold lines
and intricately detailed, giving the
clothing range an aura of carefree fun.

2

1

2

1

3

4

5

1   Plain fabrics transcend to new heights as they are embellished with jet beads and faux jewels.

2   Gut's Autumn/Winter 2008 collection revealed a dark, Gothic mood intended to exaggerate the contrast between the vivid colours and vibrant patterns.

3   The purple and gold print designed for their menswear range introduces a racy elegance to the underwear line.

4   Tight pants and loose living seemed to sum up the mood of the collection. Models wore top hats and cheetah print scarves to set a new standard for Dandyism.

5   Leather is an indispensible part of menswear in the Gut's label. Despite its significance to the fashion industry, it is rarely discussed in textile terms.

6   Everyone can be a star when wearing this print – an homage to 1970s rock star glamour.

6

2

3

Gut's is among the few textile
designers who produce designs
against a black background. 1

The label combines playful animal
forms with Victorian roses and
decorative bunting. 2

Blood-red lettering creates a
dramatic, Goth-like contrast,
as seen in this 'bleeding' motif.
The liquifying typeface appears to
dissolve, generating the effect of
dripping wax streaming down the
garment's surface. 3

The designers broke fresh
ground in the genre of animal
prints by sketching witty renderings
of fornicating sheep, copulating
dogs, and a menagerie of excited
animals. Such prints, mixing graffiti
tagging and cartoon imagery, offer
more subcultural statements than
traditional textile prints. 4

4

1 | Gut's take inspiration for their prints from rock star styles as well as Gothic lettering and subcultural slogans.

2–3 | Scribbling is often used as the basis for their motifs, with naïve line drawings overlaying elaborate patterns.

4 | Gut's cheetah fabric is worn as an accent to accessorize other items of clothing. Concealed by a knee-length dress in this image, it is an evocative reference to the animal within.

2

3

4

HANNA WERNING

Hanna Werning is based in Stockholm, but her work can be found on many continent's outside Europe. 'My prints reflect the world I live in today,' she says. 'To me, the world is like a big patchwork of different cultures, and sometimes I see my own work as a big visual collage or like the sound of a DJ sampling her own rhythms with others.'

After graduating with a degree in graphic design from Central St Martin's College of Art & Design in London, Werning established her own studio when she moved back to Sweden in 2004. Since then, she has been designing interior textiles for international brands such as IKEA and Borås Cotton, urban prints for Eastpak and Stüssy, and unique motifs for fashion labels such as Anna Sui, BoxFresh and Dagmar. Werning has also launched her own wallpaper range, which she called AnimalFlowers. Unlike ordinary wallpaper that comes in rolls, Werning's wallpaper is printed in poster format. AnimalFlowers gives consumers the freedom to buy as many individual poster sheets as they need instead of buying a whole wall roll, or to just buy single prints for framing.

Because she was educated as a graphic designer, Werning tends to describe her work in two-dimensional terms. 'I usually just call myself a designer, because I work with lots of different media,' she explains. 'However, I think one can see pretty easily that my work comes from graphic design rather than from a textile background.' Werning discovered fabric design when she was still at university, where she learned screen-printing and was drawn to making repeats rather than one-off graphics. 'I have always had a fascination for patterns, whether it is the natural pattern of wood or something more made-up and decorative,' she says. 'Textiles are interesting media to work with because they are soft and easy to mould. They follow the body of an object so nicely. I also find them interesting because they make it easy to create temporary changes in an environment, whether they are mounted on scaffolding in the city or made into a cover for a bed.'

Nature has been a constant source of inspiration for Werning, who maintains an ongoing dialogue with the natural world in her work. Her representations of animals, plant life and the landscape are drawn in fluid, organic lines, and characterized by spontaneous juxtapositions of flora and fauna. 'Taking inspiration from the landscape is second nature to me, since I grew up close to the forests,'

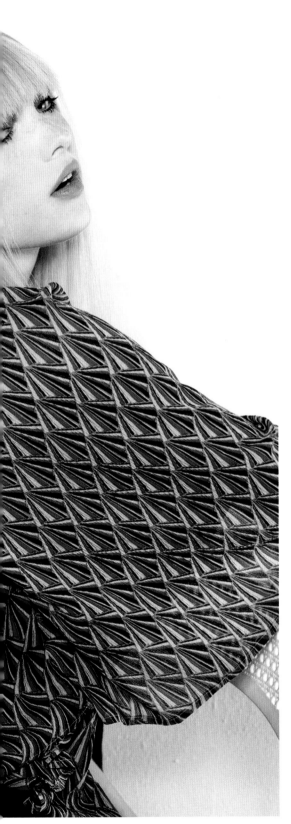

Werner explains. 'Motifs that depict nature will never go out of fashion, and they will stay with us even if technical development becomes more popular.'

Werning's prints for Swedish label Dagmar transform elements of the natural world into edgy motifs for urban fashion. Printed on silk in two colour versions, the Salmiak Pine print for Dagmar's Autumn/Winter 2006 collection repeats the graphic outline of a pine cone in sequences that recall prints of the Art Deco period. 'All of my fashion prints are made especially for the clients I work for,' Werning explains. 'I have a free hand to develop the prints as I want to. I never show a portfolio from which they can choose work. I always want to make new work for each project, because my strongest inspiration is the force of wanting to create and to develop myself. I like to challenge ways of looking at things.'

1 Designed for Swedish fashion
   brand Dagmar's Autumn/Winter
   2007 collection, Hanna Werning's
   distinctive repeated motif exuded
   heady elegance and retro style.
   This motif was printed in several
   colourways and used in the designs
   of various garments.

Werning's print for Dagmar's Spring/   1–2
Summer collection 2007 captured
the summer season in a meadow of
wildflowers against a background of
golden sunshine.

Using dark blue tones, this print   3
evokes the feeling of twilight.

One of her most popular designs,   4–6
Werning's Salmiak Pine motif,
featured in Dagmar's Autumn/
Winter 2006 collection. It was
printed on silk in two different
coloured versions.

HANNA WERNING

5

6

1-2 High-performance brand Eastpak put Werning's work to the test when they commissioned textile prints for their Spring/Summer 2006 collection. This floral motif is called Grasshopper Luck.

3-4 Also featured in the collection, this textile motif is called Ocean Star, and evokes the merging of land and sea as it depicts flora and fauna from both environments.

5 Another delicate motif created for Eastpak and taking nature as its theme, here birds fly and fish swim against a swirling current of seagrass and ripe berries. Werning named this motif Fishpond Flush.

3

4

1&4   Werning's textile prints for IKEA furniture transformed rudimentary, low-budget sofas into icons of high design. Shown here is the Ankarsvik textile print for the Klippan three-seater sofa.

2   This swatch, taken from her Wildberries textile print, reveals the elegance of Werning's intricate drawing style.

3   Her Djurträdgård, or Animal Garden, reveals the extent to which nature is a source of inspiration for Werning. Her representations of animals, plants and the natural landscape are drawn in fluid lines, and characterized by unexpected juxtapositions of flora and fauna.

5   The Fjärderlöv print embodies Werning's design philosophy in many ways. She believes that a motif must be elegant enough to sit comfortably on the body, yet dynamic enough to transform the space around it.

5

KAHORI
MAKI

Tokyo-born artist and designer Kahori Maki roots her prints in the natural world, capturing both the exotic and the everyday in stylized expressions that seem to hover between dream and reality. Few would believe that Maki's love of nature can be attributed to an earlier life sandwiched between the glass and concrete canyons of New York. 'Paradoxically, living in Manhattan made me realize how much nature pervades urban life in Japan. When I moved back to Tokyo, I rediscovered how present Shintoism is in the city. I felt like nature was a part of the human soul, something eternal, something poetic and beautiful. You could say I work in response to urban life, yet express myself by depicting nature. The extremes of nature and urban life continue to inspire my work today.'

Since she returned to Japan, Maki's prints have adorned a wide variety of media, knitting together the worlds of art, fashion and graphic design. Her work has also spun threads between Japan and the West; strands navigated with the grace of an acrobat. Installations at the ALU showroom on 24th Street and at the Location One art gallery in SoHo, where she exhibited with Yuka Honda, have showcased her unique version of the neo-gothicism gripping Japan. Maki's work is characterized by its dramatic impact: black graphics are juxtaposed against a white background, carefully drawn in swirling outlines and detailed etchings. Maki's work often features crisp outlines of verdant leaves and velvety flower petals, seductively intertwined with looping vines, forked foliage and lazy insects. 'I find beauty in things like spiders and caterpillars, forms that many would regard as grotesque or macabre,' she says. 'I can study an insect forever, noticing the gossamer textures of their wings and the soft fibres that cover their shells.'

Although most of us would regard insects as poisonous predators to be kept at a distance, Maki is not afraid to get up close. She features meandering snails that happily inhabit serpentine shells and depicts beetles with a dark lustre that evokes mystery, darkness and melancholy. Thick black strands outline the robust shapes of her caterpillars, who trail alongside weightless butterflies gently opening their wings. 'I'm not afraid of looking into the shadows and shedding light on the beautiful creatures that live in twilight worlds.'

Although Maki does not regard her figurative work to be fashion illustration, her stylized portrayals of men and women capture the essence of fashion. By suggesting the details of fashion, rather than specifically depicting garments, Maki's prints speak the language of Romanticism more articulately than they lip-sync the vernacular of surface design. Maki's elegant, reductivist aesthetic shows how unencumbered and expressive fashion figures can be, luring the viewer into a world of dreamy enchantment. Surrealism also plays a role in her figurative work: the tight curls of an afro hairstyle take the supine shapes of flower petals, and painted eye-shadow in watercolour brushstrokes completely masks the eyes.

'The figures I draw are about beauty more than anything else,' Maki explains. 'There is much more to beauty than just a look. Beauty is about elegance, style and strength, but also innocence too.' Maki's figures gaze outwards with eyes that have no pupils, a detail she likens to the slit pupils that reptiles have. 'The position of the eyes and

1   Most of Kahori Maki's inspiration comes from nature, where she finds fascination with both the exotic and the everyday. Her work is characterized by wavering, organic lines and fluid abstractions that hover between dream and reality.

the shape of the pupils may suggest how people see the world around them. Reptiles are supposed to be scary, but their eyes have an uncanny innocence about them.'

Maki made her first foray into fashion in 2005 when she was commissioned to design a repeating pattern based on an origami print, but the manufacturer thought the print was too strong for conventional clothing and rejected it. Maki shrugged off her disappointment and shifted her focus entirely on her art practice. 'I just enjoyed expressing myself as an artist generally, and then some stylists discovered my work,' Maki says. 'So, suddenly, the fashion world was inviting me to make artwork for clothing rather than a textile print, which suited me better.'

Perhaps Maki's best known fashion collaboration was with Comme des Garçons, who printed her illustrations on a special collection of transparent coats, jackets and skirts. 'I enjoyed that collaboration tremendously,' she says. 'Comme des Garçons treated my works like art and photographed them in a context that fused together fashion, fine art and graphic design.' As Maki continues to translate the fashioned body into organic forms and edgy abstractions, her work reveals the unexpected power that beauty can have.

2

2 She is one of the first fashion illustrators to identify the dramatic impact of natural forms through dark monochromes rather than more traditional soft pastels.

2

3

4

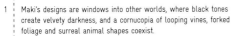

1   Maki's designs are windows into other worlds, where black tones
    create velvety darkness, and a cornucopia of looping vines, forked
    foliage and surreal animal shapes coexist.

2   Her prints feature unbroken, meandering lines that trace the outlines
    of people, animals, flora and fauna. She typically uses thick black
    strands to outline the shape of a robust shape, and delicate lines to
    depict fragile forms.

3   Some of the Maki's work features mottled brush strokes and soft
    colour tones that are reminiscent of watercolour paintings.

4   Lustrous black surfaces and the dusty, almost charred appearance
    of shadowy forms give Maki's work a subtle Gothic influence.

1-3 | Maki was commissioned by Comme des Garçons to produce designs for a limited editon of hand-printed transparent garments. She created figurative motifs that reflect a world of dreamy enchantment.

4

5

6

4 | While Maki's motifs are a hit with the fashion world as fabric prints, her work is also photoshopped into advertising imagery and painted on backdrops for fashion shoots. The art directors and stylists that she collaborates with are typically drawn to her work because of the subtle power of her black-and-white motifs.

5 | Both foreboding and engaging, this print presents shadowy surfaces streaked with sinister black veins.

6 | Dark forms set against a luminous white background to create a contrasting a feeling of lightness and weightlessness in this design.

1–2   Maki brought textile motifs and
       motor technology together in this
       car promotion, which transferred
       her print designs onto the vehicle's
       surfaces. Her prints seemed to
       dissolve the car's mass beneath a
       surface of swirling plant forms and
       striking insect motifs.

3&6   Maki has never been afraid of
       insects. Even when she was a
       child, she would marvel at the
       shiny shells of black beetles and
       sketch the delicate bodies of slow-
       moving creepy-crawlies.

4

6

5

4   This surreal hairstyle was inspired
by floral forms. The tight curls of
an afro hairstyle take the delicate
shapes of flower petals.

5   This black-and-white textile
features a repeated motif of
intertwining chrysanthemums
set within a network of foliage
and vines.

KAREN NICOL

1

2

A string of French lace winds its way through Karen Nicol's London studio, devouring plastic delphiniums, paper chrysanthemums and glow-in-the-dark jellyfish in its carnivorous wake. In the sprawl beneath it, wooden snakes slither among uncanny objects carved from dusty bones and glossy ornaments cast in coloured glass, and a centrepiece of crystal flowers, hand-painted tulips and porcelain hands nests surreally in a 1960s vase. 'I trawl flea markets, car boot sales and vintage boutiques for amazing items,' Nicol says, describing her fascination for found objects. 'That's where I look for vintage textiles, old embroideries and pieces of haberdashery, as well as things that have incredible colours, fantastic textures and interesting histories. I decorate the studio with it all, and it transforms my studio into one big mood board.'

Nicol's work can be likened to a witches' brew; an unexpected range of media and eclectic references are the magic ingredients dropped into the pot, which she later conjures forth as bewitching fabrics. 'Embroidery is a magical mix today,' Nicol says. 'It can be rooted in traditional techniques or contemporary expressions and still take textiles to the cutting edge. Thoughout my career I have found inspiration in museum collections and vintage textiles, which I then translate into contempoary fashion laterally.'

Over the years, Nicol has designed for Chloé, Givenchy and Chanel, and has developed long-standing relationships with British designers such as Betty Jackson, Clements Ribeiro, Tracy Mulligan, Matthew Williamson and Irish designer John Rocha. In recent years she has produced designs for relative newcomer, Bamford, own-label collections for British interiors company Designers Guild, plus small collections for Shabby Chic and Anthropology in the United States. 'When I collaborate with fashion designers they usually involve me at the beginning, inviting me in to look at the silhouettes they're working on, the colours they're using and the themes they are working from. They show me mood boards and fabric samples, then we discuss the scale they have in mind. I head back to my studio and start working on the embroideries. When they're ready, I go back to the designer and we photocopy them in different scales and pin them to the toiles to get an idea of what will work best. I then embroider the showpieces and follow up with the production of orders.'

1 The Honeymoon skirt takes the wearer around the world through depicting cameo panels of exotic destinations set amid foliage forms and trailing vines.

2 The Last Straw design shows the delicacy of Karen Nicol's work. Each flower is connected to the others to form the structure of the fabric.

3 Her wrap skirt designs are lavishly embroidered with intricate motifs.

4-5 Although Nicol doesn't have her own fashion label, her work is often featured on catwalks around the world. Here, her embroidery designs were commissioned by London-based design duo Clements Ribeiro for their Autumn/Winter 2004 collection.

3

4

5

Nicol's approach has often been described as 'painterly'; rather than brushing oils onto canvas, the 'paintings' she creates are produced by embroidering fabric. 'Embroidery is not limited to fabric, thread and haberdashery today,' Nicol explains. 'Things have really moved on a lot. The materials I use range from wood and paper to plastics and metal. I share my studio with my husband, the collage artist Peter Clark, who, like me, also finds inspiration in found objects.'

Nicol's materials, resources and inspirations change from season to season, because each collection she produces is shaped by her client's brief. 'Working with so many designers motivates me to think laterally so that I create completely different things for different clients,' Nicol explains. 'Every season I find myself working with new themes, sometimes even ones that oppose each other. For example, Clements Ribeiro once asked for over-the-top designs for a collection they described as "Frida Kahlo meets Singapore whorehouse", while John Rocha wanted minimal designs that evoked abstract art. Another season, two different designers, unbeknownst to each other, asked me to take inspiration from the same thing: a picture of an African boy with a tattoo on his arm. I had to take my inspiration in two very different directions so that neither designer would guess that they had given me the same brief.'

It is not unusual for Nicol to receive an intangible brief that requires her to stretch her imagination to the limit. 'One season Betty Jackson said she wanted me to visualize a scenario that would help me understand what she wanted,' Nicol says. 'So she described a railway station in the 1940s, where a beautiful young girl was saying good-bye to her lover as he boarded the train. As she waved good-bye, she was clutching a bunch of bedraggled roses he had given her. At that point Betty turned to me and said, "Karen, I want those roses!".'

1-3 | Nicol's soft furnishing fabrics for retailers such as Designers Guild and Anthropology bridge the gap between high fashion and interior design. She numbers among a handful whose work is influential in both industries.

4

5   6

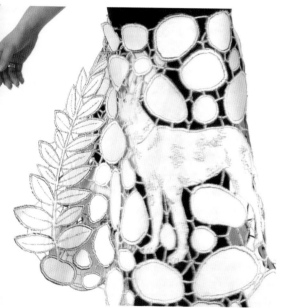

4 | Nicol's Last Straw skirt, part of a series shown previously (page 108), creates a unique silhouette on the wearer. The garments are usually worn over a dress or a pair of trousers.

5 | Dogs are a favourite motif in her work. Here, the Spot the Dog skirt features an image of a playful pet surrounded by pebble shapes and foliage forms.

6 | This Rockoko skirt is constructed from elaborate Rococco shapes. Nicol's captures the elegant curves and graceful style of the period in fabric form.

1 In this embroidered upholstery for Designers Guild, Nicol uses stark fibres to create the outlines of ethereal plant forms.

3

2

2-3 Nicol works in relief, often sculpting flower forms in dense textures that lift them above the fabric's surface and gives them a unique tactility.

4 The Kokoshka motifs feature spring flowers falling onto a table cloth.

5 This fabric for Anthropology depicts a bouquet of intricately embroidered flowers.

4

5

2
3

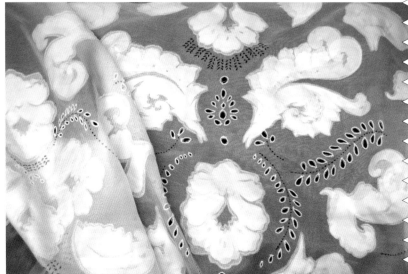

1   Nicol ventured beyond the water's edge to find jellyfish forms
    for her Plankton artwork. Their trailing tentacles are depicted
    in gossamer threads, while their translucent body mass is captured
    in loose stitches.

2   Nicol's embroidered upholstery is as beautiful for the wearer
    as her clothing.

3   A close-up of the wrap skirt shown previously (page 109) reveals
    the intricate detailing of its embroidered surface.

4   Here, Nicol perforates the surface of this diaphanous fabric with
    delicate teardrop shapes.

4

LUISA CEVESE

1-2 Luisa Cevese started her Riedizioni
     label by salvaging fabric scraps
     discarded by manufacturers and
     transforming them into a new
     material that could be used to make
     fashion accessories. As her business
     expanded she began recycling other
     materials, such as newspaper and
     printed cardboard.

Handy to use, cheap to buy and easy to dispose of, throw-away textiles once held the promise of the future. Back when Modernism kicked in, economical household scrubs, industrial filters and one-season fashion follies were considered to be hallmarks of the future. Though practical then, their legacy is tainted today; they created a generation who expected that the problems of modern life would be wiped away by disposable fabrics.

The millions of tonnes of textiles buried in landfills each year was an industry secret for several decades, a roaring white elephant in the room that manufacturers muffled and ignored. The silence was broken when Luisa Cevese, formerly a chief designer in the textile industry, revealed that the fabric remnants regarded as 'waste' by luxury manufacturers could be reclaimed and recycled. 'When I worked for a major Italian textile mill, I was discouraged by how many textiles got thrown away,' Cevese says. 'Raw edging, selvedges, scraps and seconds had no value. They just created a big mess.'

Out of the chaos of waste came the poetry of order when Cevese began reclaiming fabric scraps and exploring new ways of using them. 'I started gathering textile remnants in various places,' Cevese explains. 'Not just at the factories where they were discarded in bulk, but from families who were throwing things away, vintage textile businesses and even flea markets. My objective was to find the simplest solution which, in the widest possible sense, involved the minimum amount of waste.'

Cevese's career was not always strictly as a textile designer; for many years she headed research and development at one of Italy's largest manufacturers. 'When I realized what a big problem textile waste was I looked deeper into it, of course, using research methods to find the solution,' Cevese explains. 'Don't be misled to think into thinking that there was a huge mountain of remnants waiting to be recycled and once they were reused the problem would go away. I saw how consistent the textile waste was. Constant. I realized what was needed was an ongoing design project that would continuously recycle the wastage. That is what led me to realize that fabric scraps could be used as a basic material in manufacturing and then I started thinking about what could be made from them.'

When she was developing the prototypes that she later based her collections on, Cevese looked into combining the remnants with other materials. 'I started to combine the textile waste with plastic of different kinds,' she explains, 'and in this new hybrid plastic/fabric material I saw tremendous opportunity for development which neither a textile manufacturer nor plastic producing company could fully exploit. To my astonishment, I realized how little wastage there is in plastic production. Plastic products are made very specifically with little excess material. Anything that is left over is usually melted right back into the mix.'

Cevese founded her company, Luisa Cevese Riedizioni, in Milan, where she set up a studio and showroom and established a small factory where the remnants could be processed. 'Apart from the trash collectors, my business must have been one of the first companies in Italy to use waste as its starting point,' laughs Cevese. 'To begin with, we got leftover silk used in tie making, because the colours were so vibrant and the combinations were so unique. I then named the new material created from combining textiles and plastic "11". All I did to make it was combine "1" material with "1" more material. So in this case, 1 plus 1 is not 2; it's a third material, and so it's called 11. The next step was to start training other workers to assemble the remnants into products. I told every one of them to "express yourself", because every product has to be unique. Individual creativity is essential, because my goal is to truly melt craft and art together into products that can be made in multiples, yet in pieces that will be completely unique.'

Cevese's signature product is probably the striped tote bag for which she became famous. The fabric remnants used in the bags are arranged in horizontal lines; co-ordinated like an outfit, they are ready to be worn. Her accessory range includes pouches, purses, toiletry cases and even an iPod holder. She has also launched collections of tableware and limited-edition wall hangings made from squares of reclaimed silks found in India. Mosaic-like panels are created from vintage place mats, squares of cottons, linens and lace embroideries. Although they are pieced together simply like patchwork, the principles underpinning them – like the rest of Cevese's work – weave an elaborate model web of sustainable design.

1-3 Many of her bags are made from
discarded fashion textiles. Shredded
silk selvedges are popular because
they create a fringed effect. Cevese
cites leftover silk from necktie
manufacturers as a particular
favourite, because the colours are
especially vibrant and the colour
combinations are quite unique.

1

3

2

4 Cevese promotes large shopping bags like this as a means of minimizing plastic waste. She encourages customers to use them on shopping trips instead of the polyethylene bags supplied by most retailers.

MÁRCIA GANEM

If Márcia Ganem heard other designers complaining about how expensive materials are, she would probably laugh out loud. While many of her colleagues are likely to lavish money on overpriced silks, expensive beads and exclusive leathers, the materials Ganem uses are nothing less than priceless. In her accomplished hands, the precious gems, polished stones, facet-cut crystals and pieces of pure gold harvested from the Brazilian landscape provide a rich resource of untainted colours and original shapes. Combined with reclaimed materials and natural fibres, and crafted in the traditional textile techniques characteristic of Brazil's Bahia region, Ganem's designs are an extraordinary mix of cultural references and sustainable resources.

'The foundation of my work is the dynamic that brings textiles into dialogue with fashion, art and jewellery,' Ganem says. 'By developing new techniques, rediscovering traditional crafts and finding ways to use raw materials, I can approach fashion textiles in an innovative way.' One of the best examples of Ganem's creative process is how she took inspiration from the Xequere, a percussion instrument made from a dried gourd strung with a knotted weft, to create a new way of making a textile. 'I developed a method of making a knotted weft from polyamide fibres which I studded with gems and adapted for clothes. The textile is knotted by hand over a dress form, so you can imagine it took a lot of time and energy to perfect the technique of making it. But it was worth it, because now I can truly fuse fashion and jewellery.' Ganem famously used the technique to create a dress embedded with 7,200 carats of polished citrine, each anchored to the dress in a setting crafted from pure gold.

Ganem broke new ground when she developed methods of recycling synthetic polyamide fibres. Polyamide was originally used in the automotive industry, and Ganem was drawn to it because it has the tenacity of coconut fibre but is even easier to work with. 'Polyamide is easy to recycle and excellent to work with, so it became the base material for the textiles used to produce my couture line,' she says. 'It's easy to create a surface with it by using handcraft techniques. The appeal of the couture range isn't just that the garments are meticulously fitted, it's also because the fabrics themselves are made by hand.'

Ganem's designs could be mistaken for pure luxury, but every aspect of her production is rooted in regenerating artisan co-operatives and traditional handcraft associations. Taking the artisans' time-honoured techniques as her starting point, Ganem often introduces them to new types of material and finds contemporary expressions for their traditional crafts. Almost every collection explores a new technique, which, in turn, creates opportunities and sustainable ventures for the communities. 'My Dândi collection, from Autumn/Winter 2006, used techniques such as macramé, *nhaduti*, bobbin lace and knotted-weft. The textiles were produced in partnership with artisan communities such as the group of embroiderers known as *25 de Junho*, and a group of women from Saubara who formed a 120-member association of lacemakers. For the Dândi collection, they combined traditional bobbin-lace techniques with polyamide fibres. I believe that working with the textile traditions from the northeast in this way maintains a link between modern innovation and Brazilian cultural identity, and, at the same time, it sustains marginalized communities.'

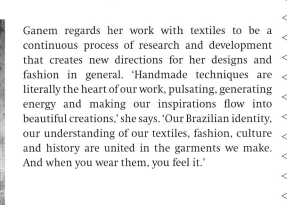

Ganem regards her work with textiles to be a continuous process of research and development that creates new directions for her designs and fashion in general. 'Handmade techniques are literally the heart of our work, pulsating, generating energy and making our inspirations flow into beautiful creations,' she says. 'Our Brazilian identity, our understanding of our textiles, fashion, culture and history are united in the garments we make. And when you wear them, you feel it.'

2

3

1   Márcia Ganem conceived this dress and fabric design as one. Hundreds of sparkling citrine crystals were knotted into polyamide fibres and woven into a unique couture creation.

2–3   Her signature Flor da Maré (Tide's Flower) piece is a uniquely semi-transparent textile with a softly textured surface. The fabric can be cut on the bias to create plunging necklines as seen in this 'vertical' tunic (2) and wrap dress (3).

3

4

1   Ganem's wedding gowns are made
      from different types of lace that
      she commissions from artisans in
      northern Brazil. This dress features
      traditional and new lace designs.

2&4   The Tide's Flower fabric shown
      previously (page 121), is made
      into a double-breasted jacket with
      a mandarin collar and a simple,
      sleeveless blouse.

3   Designed for the Spring/Summer
      2008 collection, this top combines
      Ganem's artisan lace with semi-
      precious gemstones strung on
      polyamide filaments.

1 Ganem combines fashion, jewellery design and textile techniques in a single expression in this lace and gemstone dress.

2 This 'gem' of a swimsuit has more in common with jewellery than it does fashion. The fabric is made from semi-precious gemstones strung together with natural fibres.

3 This sleeveless top is made from loosely-woven natural fibres. The design culminates in an undulating Golla collar.

3

1 Ganem's garments are often
   inspired by the textiles she creates.
   This soft, weightless fabric has
   naturally been transformed into
   a lightweight summer piece
   of clothing.

2 Made from fabric resembling water
   drops caught in a spider's web,
   this long-sleeved cocktail dress
   is made from black crystals
   strung between polyamide fibres.

1

2

Ganem's Broto dress is custom-made. It is unique in couture because the fabric, as well as the dress, are designed specifically for the wearer. | 3

This simple waistcoat is crafted from Ganem's signature lace. | 4

3

4

NATALIE CHANIN

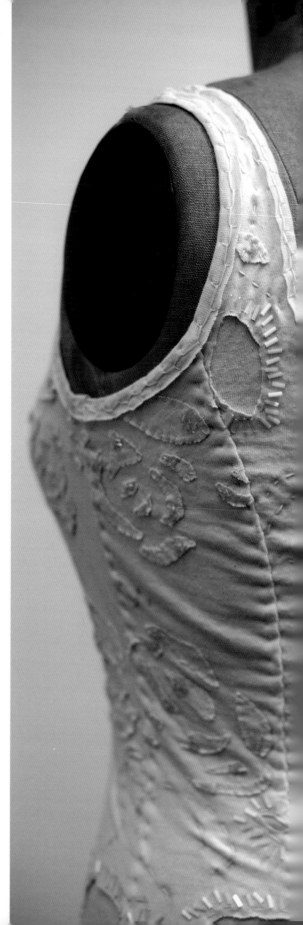

Natalie Chanin's story is no longer her own. Many Americans have now heard about the girl from rural Alabama who studied fashion, lived in Europe for ten years and returned to New York to become an overnight success. They know that her clothing is couture and that her standards are ethical – too ethical, in fact, to be produced under sweatshop conditions. Accounts of her commitment to sustainable methods have rippled through the fashion world and far beyond, where her model of using reclaimed textiles as a source material has sparked new ways of working.

Desperation drove Chanin back home to Alabama, because that was the only place she could think of where there were groups of women who could sew. 'I couldn't find people to hand-sew the samples for fashion week, and the deadline was looming,' she says. 'I came home and placed an ad in the local newspaper to find seamstresses. I had practically forgotten how in the South women of all ages get together and form sewing circles, where they socialize, sew, swap stories and teach each other techniques.' Realizing what a unique labour force she had tapped into, and that she could distribute her collections just as easily from the South, Chanin took over a rural three-bedroom ranch-style house on County Road 200 in Florence, Alabama, and relocated her business there.

'I moved back home and Project Alabama was born as a label, but almost immediately evolved into a widespread community of women,' Chanin says. 'Women of all ages, all walks of life and all interests sew my clothes. There are retired ladies working for me because they like to stay active. There are women in full-time employment who sew during their lunch breaks and free time to earn money for their kids' education. There are college students who sew to support themselves while they study. And the range of skills they have are amazing. I can give you several examples where three generations of the same family are sewing my clothes, and the older generation thinks that it's just as cool as their granddaughters do.'

One of the first challenges Chanin faced was finding a way to employ her staff legally so that they could receive benefits. 'The US has some complex labour laws which were established for good reasons, so women and children couldn't be exploited,' she says. 'To comply with the laws, we had to set up a system whereby women could

1 Recycling fabric scraps as pieces of appliqué is a fun and efficient way of giving new life to loved items of clothing. Natalie Chanin literally transforms rags to riches as she crafts couture garments from clothing cast-offs.

2 This close-up reveals how intricately her garments are hand-stitched and embroidered. The designer likes to focus on good wishes when threading the needle, encouraging seamstresses to 'use your thread to add love to what you sew'.

own their own businesses and work from home. Technically, they are contractors who use cottage industry standards for the work they do and the businesses they run. I am proud of this system and it has been wonderful to see how these women have taken their businesses into their own hands.'

Because Chanin's designs are mostly made from recycled T-shirts, the seamstresses have a unique material to work with. 'We buy reclaimed T-shirts in bulk, cut the sleeves off and open the seams to have a fabric length to work with,' Chanin explains, 'which on average measures around 76cm x 91cm (30in x 36in). Then we make garments out of them and sew on appliqués that are also cut out of T-shirt fabric. Every part of the process is done by hand and, as a result, there is hardly any waste at all.'

As well as fashion credibility, Chanin has amassed great expertise in environmental awareness and sustainable solutions. 'You know, taking cast-off clothing and transforming it into beautiful garments is something rare in the fashion world,' she says, 'but in Alabama, clothing has been recycled for several generations. Down here, even sackcloth was printed and made into clothing. Historically, Alabama was a poor area. There were never any leftovers to throw away. Not only did my grandmother not have a garbage can, she didn't even have the words in her vocabulary. Throwing something away was unheard of.'

Chanin connects locally and globally with other individuals committed to conserving resources and eliminating waste. 'Someone once criticized us by saying that it sounds like we're trying to recreate our grandmother's lives,' she says. 'I don't want to do that because without UPS, Fed-Ex, the Internet and my iPhone, I couldn't distribute my work globally from here. But my grandparents were the most sustainable people I ever met; they grew their own food and recycled everything. My grandmother once said that she was poor but she didn't know it, because there was always just enough of everything to go around. So here I am, two generations later, at a time when the United States has become the world's biggest exporter of garbage. I'm doing what I can to recycle a small part of it.'

Despite the inexpensive base materials she uses, Chanin's clothes are expensive to buy. 'Our labour overheads are huge compared to the cost of producing in the Far East, but the quality is higher and it sustains local women economically,' she says. 'I don't think that my business model is necessarily the best one for a sustainable business because relatively few people can afford my products. However, I'm doing something about that. I'm publishing a book that teaches people how to make our best-selling items themselves. I tell them that if they can't afford to buy one of my garments, buy the book and read how to make it. If they don't know how to sew, they can source some recycled fabric locally and pay someone in the community to make it.'

In 2006, Chanin decided to move in a new direction and subsequently closed Project Alabama but let her former business partner take over the name. 'My new label and I are not involved in Project Alabama at all. The label is called Alabama Chanin and I've added a jewellery line and a home collection to my range,' she explains. 'I've developed a completely new way of producing my designs. I make a series of "bodies" each season in sizes ranging from extra-small to extra-large, and produce swatch books of sample fabrics. The retailers can then choose what they think their customers will buy and place an order, or request bodies for their customers to try on and let them choose the fabric styles themselves. The long dresses have to be made from new T-shirt jersey but the appliqué is still recycled.'

People often ask Chanin what she finds rewarding about her job or what she likes best about the unique fashion collection she has launched. Irrespective of how they ask, the answer is always the same: 'I like it because it doesn't matter if someone doesn't want it or if one of the seamstresses makes a mistake. After all, it's just T-shirts we're talking about here.'

2

5

6

1   Chanin's early base fabrics were made by piecing salvaged T-shirts
     together. Today, she uses organic cotton jersey for her couture
     collection, as in this dress.

2   The designer expertly stitched the motif to appear on both
     sides of this fabric, creating a reversible hand-crafted garment.

3   She embroiders her garments with fabric scraps to create repeating
     motifs and unique patterns.

4   Recycled woven and printed textiles are often used in her work.

5   As the reverse appliqué technique forms outlines around each
     shape, it also creates a rich texture on the garment's surface.

6   Seed beads are embroidered around the folded outlines
     to enhance them.

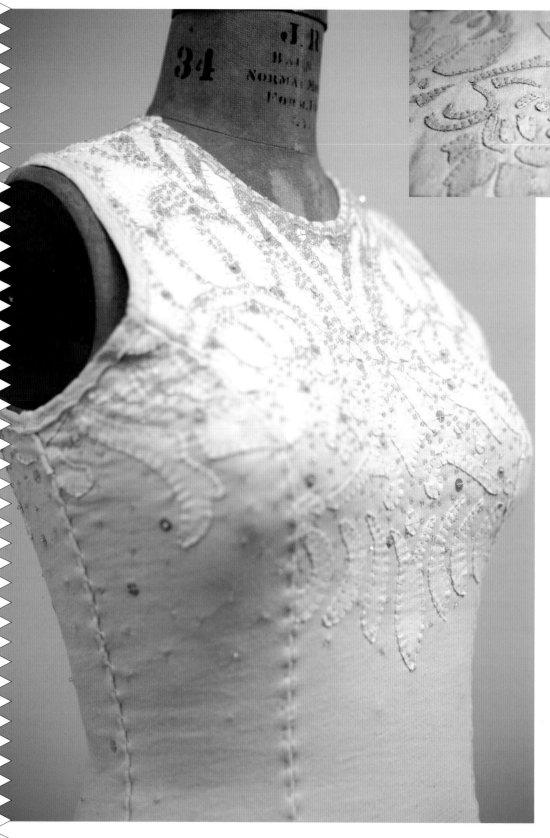

2

3

1 | Chanin's designs are some of the most lavishly-embellished garments to be made from recycled materials.

2 | Many hours of work are devoted to each fabric, resulting in a level of craftsmanship rarely found in the fashion world today.

3 | Chanin's dresses often feature cut reverse appliqués that she embellishes with glass bugle beads or seed beads.

4 | Here, individually hand-dyed repeats are embellished with seams and stitched lines to create a leaf motif.

5 | This close-up reveals how a variety of techniques are combined to create a single design. 'Spot' dying, random stitching and elegant beadwork come together to create a harmonious whole.

4

5

1   This detail reveals how nuanced
and layered Chanin's designs can be.
Quilting techniques borrowed from
traditional southern quilt-making
underpin most of her output.
Pieces of appliqué and embroidery
embellish the garment's surface.

2   Chanin's fashion accessories
combine sewing techniques with
jewellery-making skills.

2

3　This classic 'corset' design is available for anyone to recreate – the pattern is featured in Chanin's 'Alabama Stitch Book', published in 2008.

4　By using fabric scraps rather than clasps, Chanin makes jewellery that doesn't require soldering.

5　Simple, double-tied bows are a recurrent theme in her work.

Following in the footsteps of many other successful fashion designers, Chanin launched a jewellery line that embodies her unique fusion of materials and techniques. | 1

In the designer's hands, fabric scraps are easily sculpted into roses and other floral shapes. | 2-3

Chanin reclaimed discarded ladder-back chairs and gave them new life with woven fabric seats made of recycled silk neckties and shredded cotton. | 4

SÉBASTIEN BARILLEAU

1

Some objects should be handled with care. Precious crystals, priceless jewels, delicate pearls and rare silks are among these, and so are the exquisite embroideries that pass through the hands of Sébastien Barilleau, director of Cécile Henri Atelier in Paris. It is easy to talk about Barilleau's work and luxurious materials in the same breath, because most of the time, they are one and the same.

Since seizing the helm of Cécile Henri Atelier, the esteemed handcrafted embroidery studio founded by Cécile Lesage and Henri Roche, Barilleau says his life has been like living in a fairy tale. 'Being hired to lead Cécile Henri Atelier was a thrilling adventure I could not even have dreamed of,' Barilleau says. 'My job has real magic. Some of the work commissioned from us is so beautiful, so exquisitely crafted, that it takes several hundred working hours to produce it. Sometimes, when the dresses are picked up by the maisons de haute couture, I could easily imagine that they are being despatched to a fairy-tale princess, for a wedding that will take place in a palace built especially for the occasion.'

With haute couture clients such as Christian Dior, Chanel, Christian Lacroix, Givenchy, Christophe Josse, Carven, and esteemed prêt-à-porter lines by brands such as Chanel, Azzaro, Louis Vuitton, Balenciaga, Céline, Roberto Cavalli, John Galliano, Christian Louboutin and Roger Vivier, it's no surprise that Barilleau's craft is rooted in beauty and extravagance. 'Only the leading fashion brands can afford to hire us today,' Barilleau says, 'because it's only the haute couture branch of the industry that can sell clothing ornamented with rare and precious embroidery. Embroidery can be done more cheaply in foreign countries, but Cécile Henri Atelier moves forward just like its clients. Fashion and the world of luxury go very quickly, and we have know-how and creativity that mirror our client's abilities. Embroidery is not a dying art, even if very few hand-embroidery studios are left in France. In Paris, embroidery is still recognized as the rare craft that it is, an art form that still has a future.'

Barilleau heads a creative team who draw, design and dream together. 'We all work very close to each other to create a melting pot of different techniques and creativity. Sometimes we mix hand and mechanical methods. For example, Cornely is an embroidery technique using a machine operated by the embroiderer. For inlays and

1-3 To commemorate the anniversary of Thierry Mugler's Angel perfume, Barilleau and his team designed a special textile. Swarovski produced a gigantic bottle of the perfume and asked Barilleau to create a textile that could shroud the bottle in sparkling crystals. These close-ups reveal how labour-intensive its production was. The finished textile is shown overleaf (page 140).

2

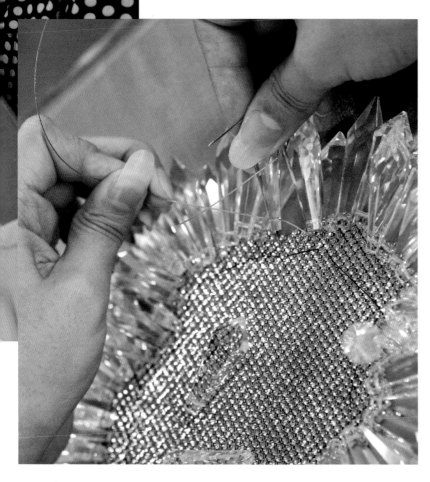

3

application we'll use a machine plate. We use various hand-embroidery techniques. La broderie à l'aiguille is a needle-embroidery method. Another one is la broderie au Lunéville, a traditional French method that uses a crochet hook. The embroiderers have to work upside down, and if the cloth is opaque, they can't even see their work.'

Although Cécile Henri Atelier's focus is primarily classic couture garments, there are also opportunities to create ground-breaking textiles. Swarovski, who had decided to commemorate the anniversary of Thierry Mugler's Angel perfume, commissioned a special textile from the studio. Swarovski had produced a gigantic bottle of the perfume, and asked Barilleau to conceive of a luxurious dress for the bottle to 'wear'. 'We were given a free hand for the creation of this project,' Barilleau explains, 'and determined the shape, the volume, the stand and the embroidery work ourselves. The one and only directive we had to follow was to use Swarovski crystals.'

Cécile Henri Atelier teamed up with Swarovski once again when they asked Barilleau to embroider Hussein Chalayan's Spring/Summer 2007 collection with conductive threads that would carry electronic signals to circuits and conductors embedded in the garments. 'It was fun to get involved with this crazy project,' Barilleau says. 'I had never seen anything like it before. The project called for hi-tech work combined with our traditional craft. On the day of the fashion show I felt lots of emotion and pride to have been requested to work on such a fantastic project. It also showed how our beautiful craft may move forward in the future as we adapt ourselves to new challenges.'

2

3

1-3 : The studio is described as 'a
melting pot of different techniques
and creativity', where hand and
mechanical methods may come
together in a single textile. The
embroiderers usually have to work
upside down, and if the cloth is
opaque, they aren't able to see
their work until they turn over the
finished textile over.

Barilleau created the embroidery for
Hussein Chalayan's Spring/Summer
2007 collection. The dresses were
stitched in 'electric' embroidery
– they required conductive threads
that would carry electronic signals to
circuits and conductors embedded in
the garments.

4-5

SHELLEY FOX

Shelley Fox is one of the most original designers on the London fashion scene today. When she launched her label in 1996, her work sparked a renewed interest in craft traditions and couture practices that inspired designers to experiment with new materials and alternative fabric cuts. Fox holds masters degrees in both fashion and textile design from Central St Martin's College of Art & Design in London, and her work shows the extent to which textile techniques can be the essence of fashion innovation. Fox's work operates like a scalpel; probing the fashioned body, she peels back the glossy skin that coats mass-production to expose the ruptures that leech the industry of its life force.

If a body without organs amounts to a human being without a soul, what would fashion be without the creative processes that drive it? A central concern for Fox is how the vast stranglehold of mass production is rapidly depriving the industry of individuality and expressiveness. 'Loom weaving, hand stitching and embroidery are vital skills that have existed for thousands of years,' Fox says. 'Yet, because more and more manufacturing is being done in the Far East, they are beginning to disappear from textile practice in Europe. Fashion isn't the same without handcrafted elements, and yet the skilled practitioners who produce original textiles and handmade pieces are having a tough time. It's been difficult for independent designers since the industry became focused on mass production. So the question I ask now is where do textile-centred designers like me go when they can't get a workforce with the sewing skills they need?'

Fox's work begins in her 'lab', an area in her studio where fabrics can be manipulated, tested, enhanced and even destroyed; some of her favourite creations are the results of lucky accidents. Manipulating and transforming fabrics enables her to work with materials not commonly used for fashion garments, and to create her own evocative textiles. 'I think being in touch with fabric development has been really important,' she says. 'I've never been satisfied with buying fabrics. There is so much of the same stuff around that it is difficult to keep an identity as a designer if you stick to mainstream fabrics.' Fox's handcrafted techniques are labour-intensive processes that can't be duplicated industrially. 'When I buy in fabrics I tend to look for classic shirtings, suitings and jerseys but always develop my own fabrics as part of the collection,' she explains.

Browsing through images taken by American photographer Walker Evans, Fox felt that the clothing captured in his documentary photographs of the Depression told a story of their own. 'What people wore had little to do with fashion by then; their clothes were threadbare and patched,' she says. 'The clothes just hung on some people because they were starving to death. There were hand-me-downs that had been taken in so drastically that the proportions didn't make sense anymore.' Haunted by what she saw, Fox began to see vintage clothing with fresh eyes. 'Each garment tells a story of its own. I was fascinated by how each alteration was visible inside. When the seams had been taken in and let out several times, the stitching showed how many. Once, I unstitched an overlocked seam to find a seam inside it that had been finished with pinking shears, so I could tell that the generation before had taken it in. That indicated that the coat had been worn for three generations of women, probably by members of the same family. I started thinking of the garment as a map that charted a shrinking waist size through the generations, then realized how seldom hand-me-downs are kept today. Usually, by the time it no longer fits, it's no longer in fashion and it just gets chucked out.'

About that time, Fox received a phone call from the British Medical Research Council, who invited her to participate in the high profile 'Nobel Textiles' project marking their 90th Anniversary. 'They paired fashion designers with Nobel laureate scientists, and I was happy to have been asked to collaborate with Sir Peter Mansfield, the scientist who invented the MRI scanner,' Fox explains. 'Right now, the MRI team at Hammersmith Hospital is pioneering new MRI scanners that map out the fat in the body's organs to determine if internal fat can have detrimental effects. They've recruited a team of volunteers that will gain weight over a six-month period so that their fat levels can be measured.'

Fox was excited by these two extremes: firstly, how clothing could record weight loss, and secondly, how technology could map weight gain. Hand-me-downs, as an analogue system, used tailoring techniques to chart substantial changes in the wearer's body, which was more or less what the ultra-modern MRI technology was doing. 'I think the way that textiles can chart these extremes is interesting,' she says, 'and I like being able to use them to bridge the distance between lo-tech and hi-tech, albeit in a symbolic way.'

Fox plans on building bridges with textiles that make craft techniques and tailoring visible; not by deconstructing them, but by reconstructing the techniques that seem to be dying out. 'I'm creating textures and motifs by using things like naïve stitching, pinking cuts and appliqués. It's hard for me to say if these textiles will build bridges or reconstruct the hand-me-down tradition, but wearing them will remind us of the secret histories that garments have long had.'

1   Shelley Fox holds MA degrees in both fashion and textile design, placing equal emphasis on both disciplines in her work. Scorched fabric became one of her trademarks early on in her career when she burned motifs into her textiles and then appliquéd melted sequins.

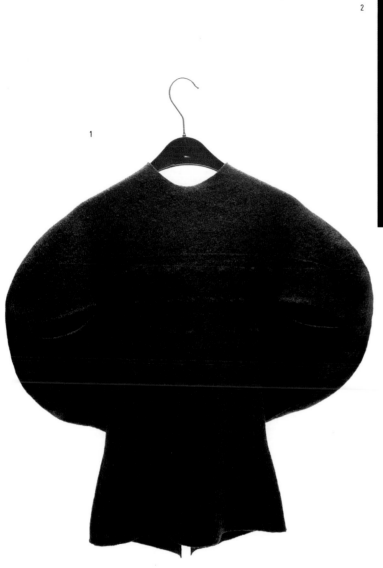

Fox sparked renewed interest in dense fabrics, such as felt, as
she reclaimed them for fashion. As used for this garment in the
Autumn/Winter 1998 collection, it gives a firm structure to create a
silhouette   shape that is independent of the body.

1

The designer often conceives fabric, form and surface motif as a
single expression. Fox's garment designs are rarely 'immediate';
these pieces for her Negative collection in 2006 slowly unravel as
the wearer moves, to reveal unexpected motifs.

2&6

3-4 : The unstructured drapery Fox used
for this garment, also designed for
her Negative collection, used an
array of sheer fabrics to create
a lightweight, voluminous dress.

5 : This trouser ensemble, for the
same collection, cuts away panels
of fabrics to reveal motifs hidden
in the lining underneath.

4

5

6

3

1&4 Fox's Autumn/Winter 2000
collection was unique in it's use
of structured textiles and hand
processed fabrics. She deployed
a delicate balance of couture
techniques and craft practices to
create an edgy, elegant collection.

2–3 The Spring/Summer 2003
collection was inspired by a range
of quirky textiles. Shapes of dinner
napkins, taken from a variety of
restaurants, and pillowcases made
for international airlines, were
reconfigured into striking garments.

2

4

5 Discarded fabrics and reclaimed clothing have long fascinated Fox, as she looks for tailoring details or embroidery stitches to tell the story of the garment.

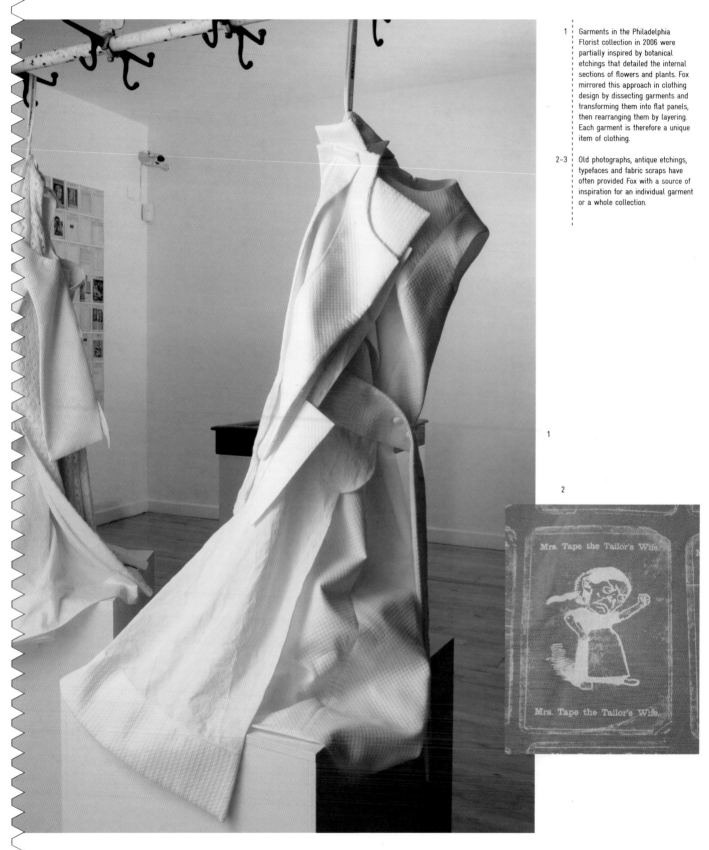

1   Garments in the Philadelphia Florist collection in 2006 were partially inspired by botanical etchings that detailed the internal sections of flowers and plants. Fox mirrored this approach in clothing design by dissecting garments and transforming them into flat panels, then rearranging them by layering. Each garment is therefore a unique item of clothing.

2–3   Old photographs, antique etchings, typefaces and fabric scraps have often provided Fox with a source of inspiration for an individual garment or a whole collection.

1

2

Mrs. Tape the Tailor's Wife.

Mrs. Tape the Tailor's Wife.

H E

S

T

HERE

THERE

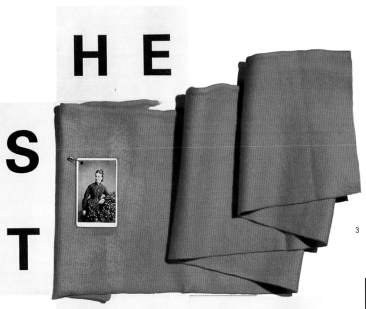

3

4 | Fox was acclaimed for her costume designs for the Michael Clark Dance Company.

5 | The Autumn/Winter 2001 collection featured a mixture of silk, jersey and cableknit fabrics. This skirt featured a Scribble motif drawn by hand and configured into a pattern repeat.

5

4

1   Fox finds beauty in unexpected forms. Her unusual motifs often result from experimentation in which her fabrics can be manipulated, deconstructed and even destroyed; some of her favourite creations are the results of lucky accidents. She literally 'played with fire' to create the scorched motif for this skirt.

2–4   These designs for Fox's Spring/Summer 2002 collection were inspired by the crispness of paper cut-outs. The designer used details from antique Georgian maps and old sepia-coloured photographs to create surface motifs for them.

2

4

3

1 Fox is concerned that the popularity
of mass textile production could
deprive the industry of individuality
and expressiveness. Her designs are
often crafted in local textiles that
are loom woven and hand-stitched.

2

3

4

2-4 These garments were designed for the Philadelphia Florist collection in 2006, which gave Fox new inspiration for structuring her clothing designs. She broke down the denominations that traditionally demarcate a garment's front and back, neckline and hemline, and rearranged them to create unique shapes and unexpected details.

THEA
BJERG

Silky textures, translucent surfaces and radiant colours fuse seamlessly in Thea Bjerg's forward-thinking designs, creating fabrics that are both intellectually stimulating and visually spectacular. Bjerg's fabrics are robustly textured, yet ethereally gossamer. Many have an uncanny ability to simulate new forms or just remain perfect in their original state, possessing an element of mutability that positions them somewhere between dream and reality.

It's no surprise that Bjerg is regarded as one of the most original textile designers in Denmark today. But although her work is widely varied and international in scope, it is difficult to pigeonhole Bjerg's designs or attribute them to one particular genre. Her work is neither rooted in the past nor inspired by prevailing trends, yet it articulates a moment in textile design when the boundaries between the creative disciplines are beginning to blur. Variously described as 'painterly', 'sculptural', 'fashionable' and 'architectural', Bjerg's élan lends itself to a variety of interpretations. Against the body, her fabrics fashion the wearer in textural silhouettes. Stretched over furniture or supported by free-standing frames, they assume the guise of fluid upholstery or sinuous screens. In a gallery context, her textiles occupy the visual space traditionally allocated to painting and sculpture, and they strike chords with both art forms.

In collaboration with New York's Museum of Modern Art and the Danish Crafts Council, Bjerg designed three scarves in silk and polyester organza that bridged the gap between art and commerce beautifully. Invited to produce a collection for the Biró gallery in Munich, she worked on a smaller scale to design sets of collars and cuffs. Resembling jewellery more than fashion textiles, the pieces were structured by laser cuts, hand pleating and slashing, then printed with metallic films.

For nearly two decades, Bjerg's fabrics have been formed by a wide variety of inspirations and techniques. She often merges craft techniques with industrial processes, and experiments with ultrasonic cutting and welding, laser cuts and industrial pleating have led to crepe-treated silks, spiralling scarves, heated-fused fabrics and pleated wraps. 'Much of my work is experimental,' Bjerg says. 'Mostly I think about how I can create a three-dimensional perspective on a two-dimensional fabric, and

1 Thea Bjerg's fabrics are richly textured, yet delicate and gossamer. Many of her textiles create other-worldly forms that offer the wearer the experience of existing some-where between dream and reality.

this is something that textile designers everywhere can appreciate, because we all struggle with it.'

Among Bjerg's signature motifs are witty repeats inspired by spark plugs, old medallions and classic cars printed with metallic dyes. But most of her designs are non-figurative, striking in their stylistic neutrality without being stark. At the same time, the brilliance of her colour palette gives her textiles lasting impact. Vivid Renaissance colours were a source of inspiration that led her towards rich jewel tones, while the muted colours of paintings by fifteenth-century Dutch and Italian masters come alive in her matt fabrics.

Fusing layers of cloth together gives Bjerg more substance with which to work, yet she relies on an intangible device to give her textiles a third dimension. 'I live in the northern latitudes where the sun bathes the landscape in luxuriant light,' she says. 'Nature is giving me a tool to work with. I can look at the same textile several times a day and see that it looks different in the changing light. The more textured the surface is, the more dramatic these changes are, and that's what gives the textiles life.' Bjerg's studio comes alive as the sun travels across the sky, suffusing her workspace with a kaleidoscope of motifs cast by the shadows that follow its rays. 'Choosing luminous colours and reflective surfaces enhances the impact of the light even more,' Bjerg explains. 'Matt fabrics absorb the light and give the textile a dense appearance.'

Bjerg's Aquatic collection was partly inspired by the sea creatures who use their colours and textures as a disguise or a cover-up. In certain respects, fashion textiles fulfil the same purpose; as they reveal and conceal they also function as a metaphor for the thrill of avoiding detection. 'Textiles can cover us and shroud us but they can also attract the gaze of others. This is something that I find compelling about sea life, that many of the colours and textures that draw me to them enable them to hide from other creatures.'

Although the striking beauty of Bjerg's textiles makes them unlikely hiding places, they still provide a perfect refuge. In moving fabric design away from the perception that textiles are static, lifeless entities, Bjerg lines our surroundings with subtle motifs and understated sculptural forms that outline a fresh direction for the styles of the future.

1 Bjerg often merges craft techniques with industrial processes, and experiments with ultrasonic cutting and welding, laser cuts and industrial pleating, to create new forms.

2&4 Invited to produce a collection for the Biró gallery in Munich, Bjerg worked in a small scale to design sets of collars and cuffs that were sold as jewellery.

3 She likes to study the way that ambient light is captured on the surfaces of her fabrics. 'The changing light is what brings my textiles to life.'

4

5　When worn on the body, Bjerg's fabrics fashion the wearer
in textural silhouettes.

6　Fusing layers of cloth together gives Bjerg more substance to work
with. As she juxtaposes different colours within the same surface,
she creates a colour palette that gives her designs more impact.

6

5

1-3 By harnessing the passing light
and ingeniously capturing it in folds,
textures and pleating, Bjerg invites
the viewer to caress her work
with the eye as much as with the
hand. 'Light gives all things their
presence,' she explains. 'The way
fabrics catch the light is important;
it holds the secret of its three-
dimensional appeal. I can treat
the fabric in a way that it will look
pleated in a certain light, and even
keep that shape when draped
around the body to follow the
movement of the wearer.

1

2

3

4

In order to create lasting surface   4
decoration, Bjerg moves deep
into the fabric's surface to
construct random configurations
or repeating shapes.

Playing with light and shadow   5
creates fluid textures that move
unpredictably, creating a range of
ephemeral motifs.

Berg's work takes fabric design far   6
beyond the perception that textiles
are static, lifeless entities. Her
fabrics adorn the body with subtle
motifs and understated sculptural
forms that outline a fresh direction
for the styles of the future.

6

1   The crisp folds and sharp cuts of this collar and cuff jewellery set create a dense texture. As the fabric itself is pliable and lightweight, the wearer feels as if they wear nothing at all.

2   Bjerg's Dark Black Scorpion Fish textile is crafted from polyester organza fabric. It is structured by laser-cutting, folding, stitching and hand-pleating techniques.

2

3–4 The Rose Quartz Sea Fan textile is made from glass organza, named for its transparent properties. The textile is folded and pleated by hand, and then machine-pleated.

5 The feather-like striations of Bjerg's gossamer textiles give them a floating appearance. Her wraps are said to drape around the wearer's back like angel wings.

4

3

5

1   Bjerg's fabrics have a unique translucence. The base fabrics she chooses for her pleated textiles are often diaphanous, and the tiny folds in the material's surface both capture light and defract it to create a striking texture.

2   Her fashion fabrics are often used as wraps or scarves.

3   Her handcrafted detailing can be seen in every fold of the fabrics she produces.

4   Entitled Bright Red Coral Formation, this uniquely structured textile was named after the aquatic form that inspired it. Bjerg began with silk organza and polyester organza fabrics, then dyed them red. The fabric was then cut with an ultrasonic cutter, hand-pleated, and stitched.

2

4

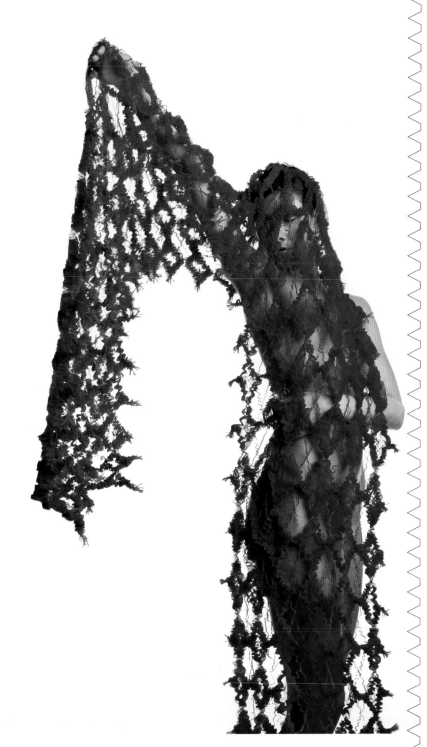

3

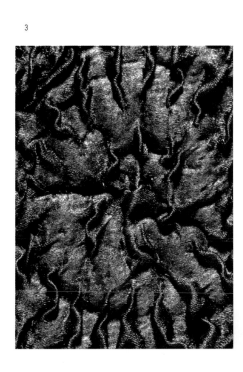

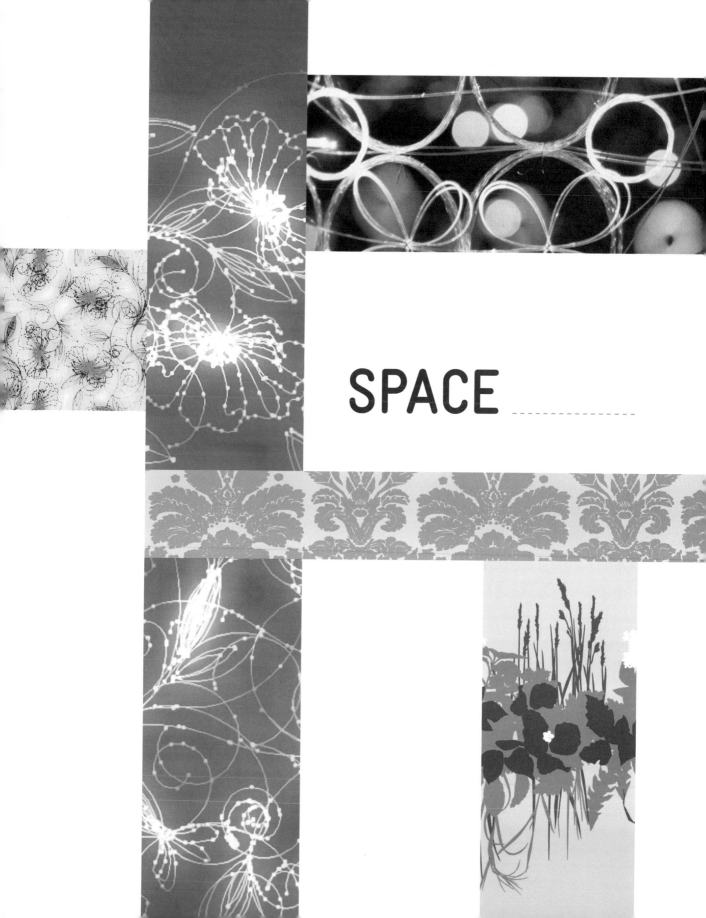

SPACE

FABRIC AS STRUCTURE AND FORM

Exciting exchanges are taking place between textiles and space. At a time when mobility, mutability and multi-functionality are becoming key considerations for urban interiors, textile designers are hitting back with fabrics that feature some of the most radical innovations in design today. Textiles are forging new relationships with the built environment, and the projects that result are striking showcases of the unique textures and tactilities that fibre-based forms can have. Textiles have always had an intrinsic ability to demarcate space, absorb sound and create decorative elements, but today they combine the poetics of art with the radical aesthetics of contemporary architecture. The beautiful structures that result often appear to transmute architectural space into urban art.

That said, the new breed of interior fabrics can no longer be described as just pretty patterns; they are hi-tech devices that transcend the decorative altogether. As digital technology equips fabrics with interfaces capable of transferring surface information, a whole new range of visual and structural effects begin to emerge. Designers can now use these programmable surfaces to achieve new levels of innovation. By adjusting and reconfiguring their patterns and colour-ways to suit individual settings, every interior can have a bespoke feel, or be redecorated at the flick of a switch.

Fabrics can be woven from fibre-optic strands, and light-emitting diodes illuminate just like any conventional textile can. Because these fibres don't emit heat, they can come into contact with the body and other textile forms without the risks associated with conventional light fixtures. When connected to sensors, LED-enhanced textiles can be programmed to respond to environmental factors, sometimes even tracking human traffic by intensifying as people move past. This new breed is sparking a process I describe as the 'furniturization of textiles'; as hi-tech fabrics begin to mimic interior accessories and pieces of furniture, they often replace them altogether.

Texture is still an important aspect of interior design, but textile practitioners are less likely to rely on surface techniques to create it. Designers working with dense materials such as felt often prefer to perforate, fold and layer a single piece of fabric rather than adding appliqué to the surface. As designers shift their focus from surface design to the fabric's structural integrity, they pioneer a new, minimalist methodology capable of creating more volume while generating less waste.

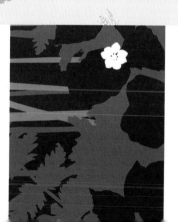

ANNE KYYRÖ QUINN

With their sleek silhouettes, minimalist motifs and textured surfaces, the fabrics designed by Anne Kyyrö Quinn are some of the most visionary expressions of interior textiles today. One of the first designers to rediscover felt and update it for the twenty-first century, Kyyrö Quinn broke fresh ground when she used the material to pioneer a striking range of interior textiles. Eschewing traditional ornamentation, Kyyrö Quinn's signature style peels away surface embellishment to expose the substance and structure that robust materials can have.

Finnish-born Kyyrö Quinn established her studio in London in 1999 with a portfolio of just six core designs and a small range of interior products. She licenced her first lighting design to Innermost, then sold interior textiles to top retailers such as Roche Bobois, Selfridges and The Conran Shop. Since then, her collection has evolved to include blinds and window screens, wall panels, table accessories and upholstery fabrics, and her consultancy portfolio has attracted a range of ground-breaking projects. De Beers Diamonds invited Kyyrö Quinn to design textile installations for their London showroom, where her designs created dramatic backdrops that echoed the facets of the cut gems, while providing textile backdrops for the set of the film *Oceans Thirteen* (directed by Steven Soderbergh and starring George Clooney and Brad Pitt) brought her designs Hollywood fame.

Collaborations with architects and interior designers has brought Kyyrö Quinn's textiles into the public eye, famously at the National Tennis Centre in Wimbledon, where she designed large-scale installations in felt. 'Working in an architectural way enables me to take natural fabrics in new directions,' she explains. 'It's so exciting when you discover how much more they can do.' Kyyrö Quinn has stretched textiles across huge surface areas to line interiors with soft inner skins, and aligned organic fabrics with hi-tech software to create enormous stage curtains and theatrical scrims. 'Irrespective of how large the surface area should be, my starting point is always the fabric's structure,' she explains, 'which I explore to see how well it holds its shape, whether it frays or not, and test how the fibres react to handling.'

Felt, in Kyyrö Quinn's hands, can be described as a miracle material. 'Felt is environmentally friendly, tactile, soft, durable and easy to work with,' she explains. 'Lengths of felt work just like other interior textiles, and often out-perform them. Thicker densities of felt possess unrivalled structure

1

2

and strength which makes them perfect for interior architecture. Because the fibres are so heavily compressed, felt is super strong, has incredible acoustic properties and can be fire-proofed like any other material.'

One of Kyyrö Quinn's first interior commissions was for a series of textile panels for a London restaurant, whose owner regarded her work to be on a par with modern painting. 'We mounted three felt panels on the wall, then noticed that it had suddenly gone quiet,' she explains. 'I was amazed at how much sound the fabrics absorbed. They immediately transformed a big, noisy area into a cosy and relaxing environment. Because of that, I realized I had stumbled upon an exciting new application for my work, and I had my textured designs tested for their acoustic properties. The Sound Research Laboratories Ltd gave me a long technical report to show my clients, then said "All you need to know madam is that they suck up sound like sponge!".'

Kyyrö Quinn traces her signature style back to her Finnish roots, attributing her clean lines and minimalist palate to her Nordic heritage. 'Finland has a deep appreciation of its design history,' she says, 'so I was fortunate to grow up understanding that good designs are long-lasting and iconic, not just short-lived trends. As a designer, I challenge myself to transform the classical materials of the past into new products for the present. As I do that, I hope to design textiles inspiring enough to forge a fresh direction for the styles of tomorrow.'

1-2 Recognizing the acoustic properties that 100% felt wool can have, Anne Kyyrö Quinn developed a range of layered textiles engineered to dampen sound or absorb it altogether. 'The surfaces of my fabrics are intricately structured,' she explains, 'which makes them highly absorptive.' Cut, sewn and finished by hand, her acoustic panels muffle noise while resonating with a buzz of their own.

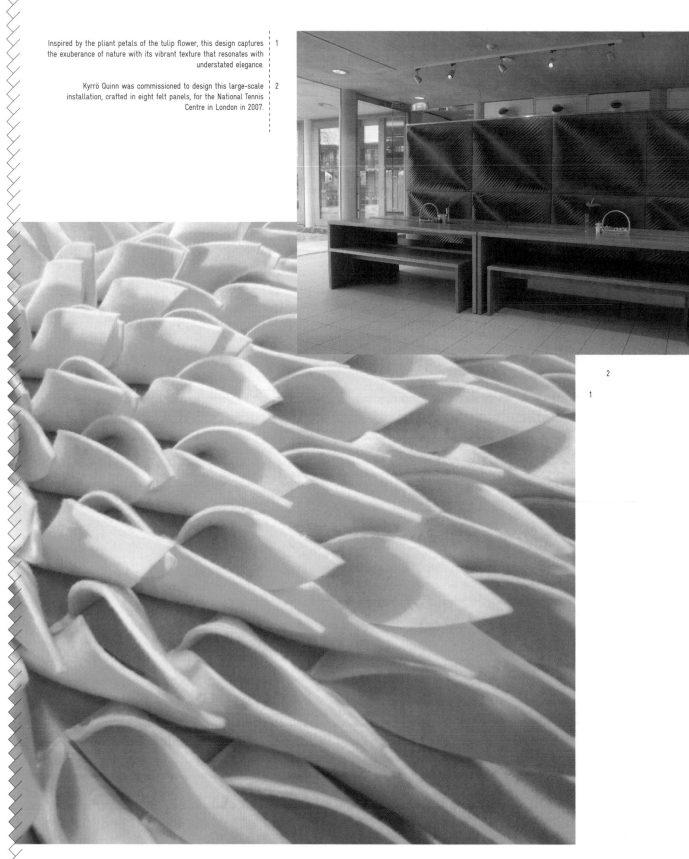

Inspired by the pliant petals of the tulip flower, this design captures the exuberance of nature with its vibrant texture that resonates with understated elegance. | 1

Kyrrö Quinn was commissioned to design this large-scale installation, crafted in eight felt panels, for the National Tennis Centre in London in 2007. | 2

2

1

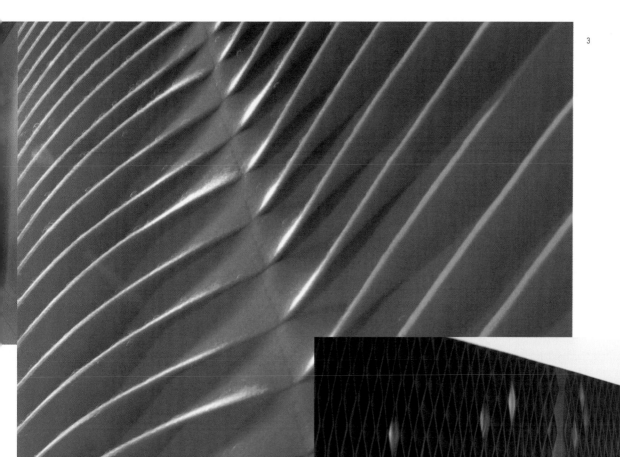

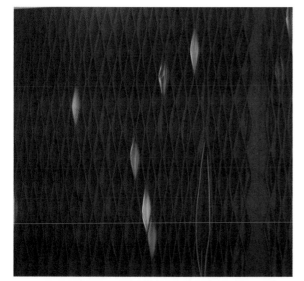

3

5

4

3 | A network of textile strands evoke the veins that trace the surfaces
of tree leaves. Sewn to a base layer of fabric underneath, they form
a pattern borrowed from one of nature's own motifs.

4-5 | Surface and structure are folded into one in this striking theatre
curtain. The textile is created by sections of pleated felt inset with
flashes of colour to enhance its diamond-like pattern.

ASTRID
KROGH

Astrid Krogh is the Penelope of our time. Like the faithful weaver depicted in Homer's *Odyssey* who wove textiles by day and unravelled them at night, Krogh's work disappears as soon as the lights are turned off.

Krogh trained at the Danmarks Designskole in Copenhagen, where she is still based today. She anchors her designs to new technologies by weaving lengths of optic strands into iridescent tapestries that glow, illuminate and flare into a rainbow of brilliant colours. 'Fibre-optic textiles are the visual pulse of life,' Krogh says. 'They are a beautiful blend of light sources. My works incorporate artificial light but they are not artificial light sources in themselves. My work is mostly influenced by the daylight I see outside my window. You could say that as my textiles become brighter, or less intense, they imitate the changes that occur in natural light throughout the day. In fact, they are never the same from one day to the next, or even from one moment to the next. The way that light plays with shadows all the time makes small changes thoughout the day, creating effects that make you open up your eyes.'

Whether seen in the cold light of day or in the dreamscapes of night, Krogh's works always blur the boundaries between art, technology and textile design. 'Working as a textile designer gives me a huge field to play around in,' she says. 'Fibres can conduct light, but there are also fibres that can be used inside the human body, and textiles that can extinguish fires as well as be buried under the earth to prevent erosion. I can also work like a contemporary artist, using my textile training to create light installations.'

Most of Krogh's projects are made for the interior, but some of them are designed for the façade. Her work seems to mark a transitional space between the inside and outside world, charting a course that may only be visible in darkness. 'That is the reality of textiles today,' she explains. 'They are a rich and diverse material that holds new possibilities for all aspects of contemporary architecture. My starting point, as a textile designer, is to identify how each place or individual room has its own atmosphere. I have to find out what makes the place special, or decide what I need to do to make it special. If my work is commissioned for an old building, I may take an aspect of its history and use it in a contemporary context. Or, if it is a new building, I try to understand the architecture and relate my work to it. In each case I build models of the room or the building to recreate the physical feeling of the design. I almost always try it out by creating a 1:1 scale to test how the light and materials will react in reality.'

Although Krogh works with hi-tech materials, she relies on traditional techniques to craft her textiles. 'It is very important to me to be able to switch between old craft techniques and new technologies,' Krogh explains, 'because I am highly inspired by both. I'm not working with silk, wool and linen, I'm working with highly advanced fibres. Yet, the simple weaving techniques that craft my textiles are more or less the same. I find it fascinating that we rely on old craftsmanship to take new materials to the cutting edge. There is a future to be fulfilled and new possibilities to meet. I consider that to be a gift, and a challenge.'

1 Krogh's Holbein tapestry was inspired by the geometrical motifs that characterize traditional kelim carpets. She outlined similar shapes with colourful neon tubes to create a luminous textile form.

2 This detail from Astrid Krogh's Flora motif is an architectural 'embroidery' created by threading neon tubes along the surface of a building.

3 Waltzing is a luminous tapestry that combines textile traditions with modern technology. The LED lighting sequences change randomly to constantly form new patterns.

3

2

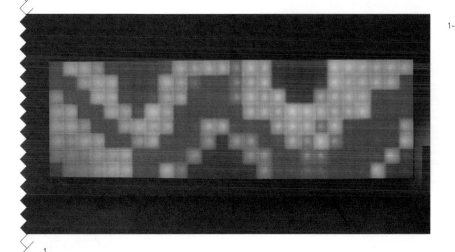

1–3 Waltzing, shown previously (page 173), is a large-scale vertical tapestry measuring 2.10m x 6.8m x 20cm (6.9ft x 22.4ft x 7.9in). Its motifs were inspired by Ikat fabrics, and its lighting technology reconfigures them into new, constantly-changing patterns. Each remains on view for four seconds, then, over an eight-second sequence, morphs into a new one. The tapestry becomes interactive when linked to a floor mat that enables viewers to control the patterns by the movement of their feet.

1

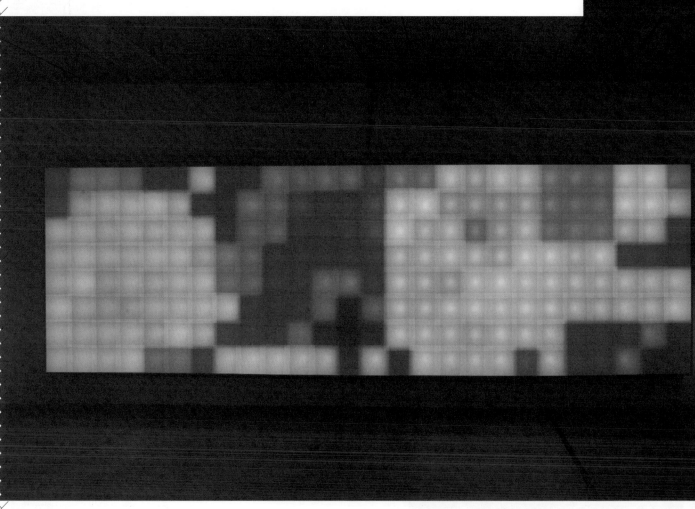

2

3

4

The same tapestry consists of
26 x 8 LEDs backlit by light-
emitting diodes (LEDs) programmed
to fade, brighten and pulsate. LEDs
use less energy than regular bulbs,
and so conserve more electricity
than other light sources, an
important consideration for Krogh.

4

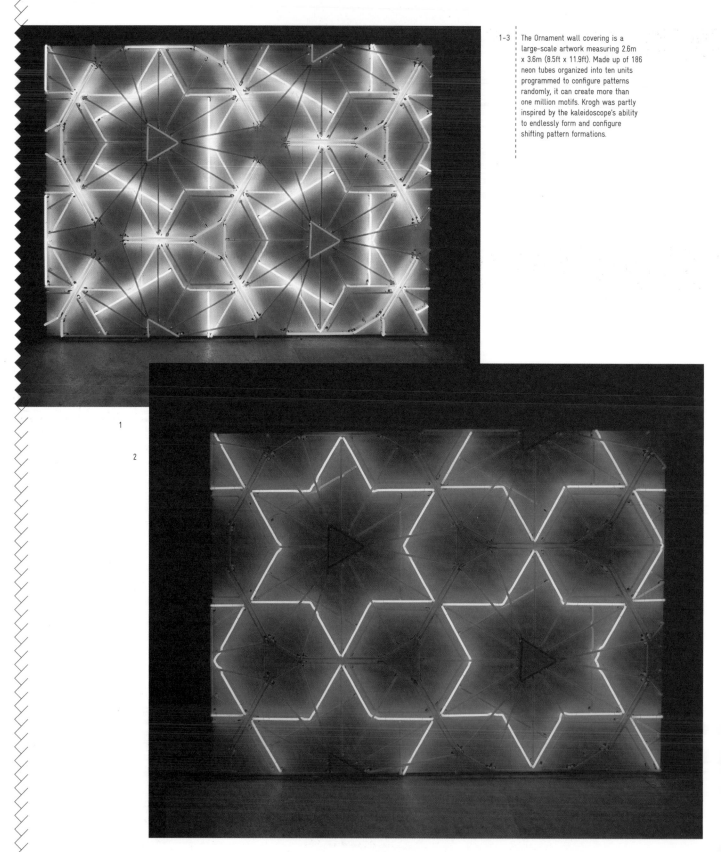

1–3 The Ornament wall covering is a large-scale artwork measuring 2.6m x 3.6m (8.5ft x 11.9ft). Made up of 186 neon tubes organized into ten units programmed to configure patterns randomly, it can create more than one million motifs. Krogh was partly inspired by the kaleidoscope's ability to endlessly form and configure shifting pattern formations.

1

2

3

4 Krogh's work blurs the boundaries
   between art, textiles and technology.
   Her textile background enables her
   to relate fabric design to site-specific
   spaces, while her imagination inspires
   her to work like an artist.

4

1

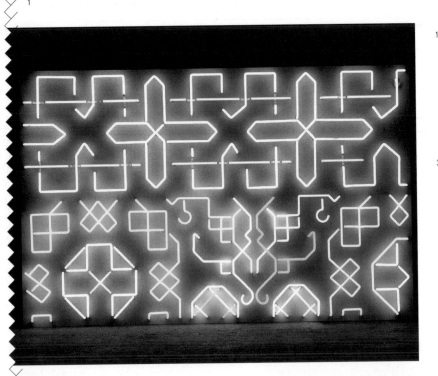

2

1-2　This large-scale neon wall-hanging was commissioned by the Danish Parliament, so Krogh aptly named it Polytics. It fulfils a request for a design that would bring light and colour to one of the parliament building's long, dark corridors. As Krogh interweaves neon tubes, she mimics textile production. Each individual neon tube represents a single stitch.

3-4　Krogh's clients usually commission site-specific work from her, requiring her to think like an architect in order to make a response to pre-existing surfaces and built structures. Her works are uniquely suited to both indoor and outdoor spaces.

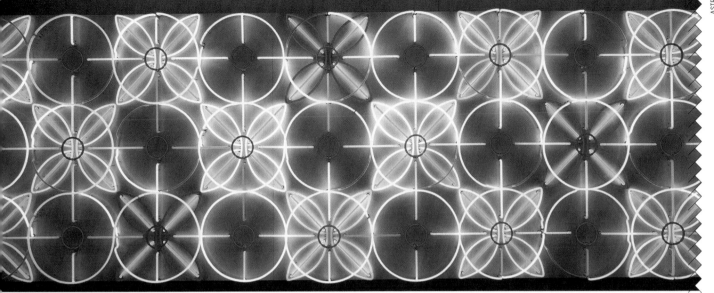

3

4

1–2 This textile is 14 metres
(46 feet) high, rising vertically
through several storeys of a
corporate building in Copenhagen.
Constructed from a woven steel
mesh, the installation was
conceived as a textile wall that
could absorb ambient noise in the
space. By day, the neon lights fade
to grey against the surface of the
steel mesh. At dusk, they morph
into vivid colours that can be seen
clearly from the street outside.

1

2

3

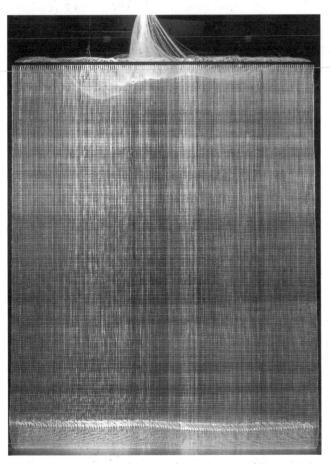

4

3&5 The Flora motif shown previously (page 173) was designed in
2007 in response to a commission from the city council in Kolding,
Denmark. Here, neon tubes are used to embroider the external
surface of a historic building, where they ornament the structure by
day and create a spectacular light show at night. It took 220 metres
(722 feet) of neon tubing to cover the wall.

4 Krogh's Blue textile is made from optic fibres. Thin and pliable, she
can weave them on a conventional loom. The textile changes colour
constantly, morphing from sky blue to azure, then from cobalt to
deep blue.

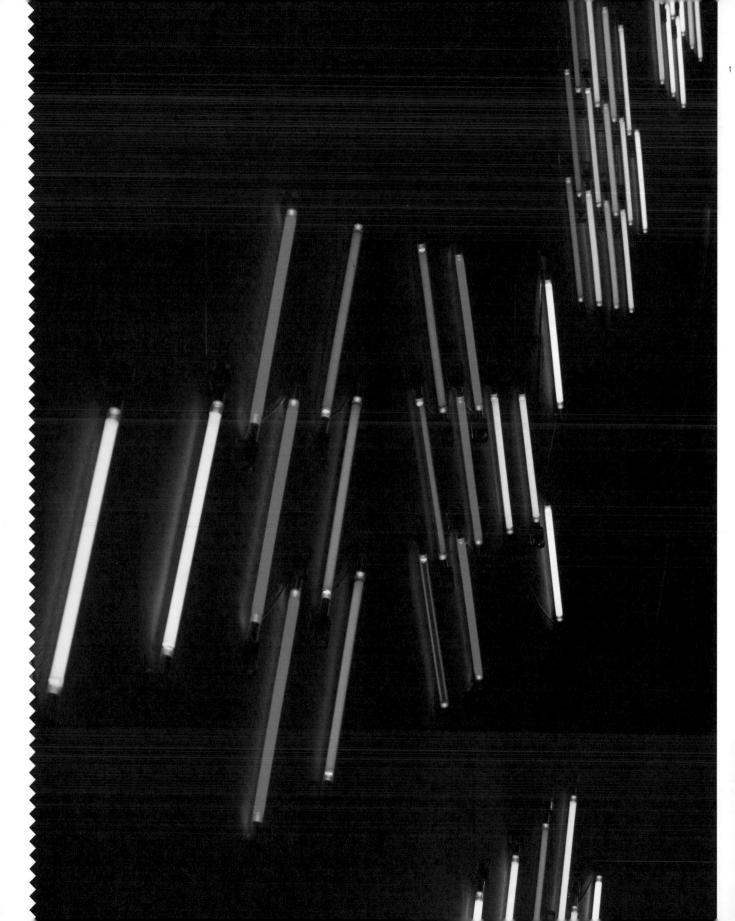

3

2

FOYER

1-3 | This wall motif was designed in
2005 for Næstved's Culture Centre
in Denmark. Rather than design
a conventional wall-hanging or a
mural, Krogh created an eye-catching
installation by using neon tubes
and mirrors. The staircase links
two separate parts of the building;
regarding it as a transitional space,
she created a motif that would evoke
movement and provide a visual
bridge between the two areas.

CAMILLA
DIEDRICH

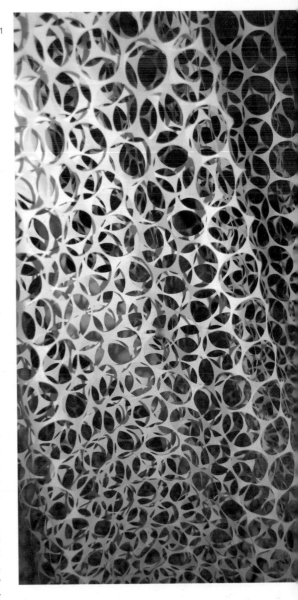

Swedish designer Camilla Diedrich may look like an anarchist, but she thinks like an architect. One of the first textile designers to start cutting holes in textiles and structuring them in terms of negative space, Diedrich's early works related more to deconstruction architecture than they did to fabric design. 'I've always liked surfaces,' she says. 'They are what we see first, what invites us closer and what draws us in.' Diedrich's talent for laser-cutting circular repeats and crescent shapes imbues her works with the transparency, texture and robustness more typical of a building façade than a fabric length. Her work transforms flat surfaces into richly-textured, three-dimensional forms that challenge conventional ideas of what a textile should be.

Despite her fascination with surfaces, there is nothing superficial about Diedrich's work. From her studio in Stockholm, she produces an extensive range of wall hangings, pendant lamps and minimalist room dividers, manufactured in synthetic fabrics and processed materials. Her laser designs, such as her ground-breaking AHIT fabric, are actually collages of cuts formed through computer-automated cut-outs. Diedrich uses lasers to create circular shapes and spiralling patterns, or perforates fabrics with small holes to make them semi-transparent.

All that Diedrich is today can be attributed to her education at the University College of Arts, Crafts and Design in Stockholm. Not because of what the professors taught her, but because of what they failed to teach. 'My tutors never understood what I was doing,' Diedrich explains. 'My extreme ideas were considered to be anarchy. They really complained about my approach and said I had no future. But even as a student I understood that you had to pioneer new approaches to get ahead, because the textile industry is flooded with designers who only learn pattern design.' What Diedrich couldn't find in her Swedish education, she looked for abroad. She was especially drawn to the Japanese tradition. 'I was really inspired by a course in Shibori, because it created unique patterns rather than a series of repeats.'

Her decision to move away from traditional patterns was reinforced by a conversation Diedrich overheard outside the textile gallery at a design exhibition. 'As two people walked past, one of them said "they're exhibiting textiles

1   Camilla Diedrich was one of the first designers to structure interior textiles in terms of negative space. Her groundbreaking AHIT fabric has more holes in the surface area than fabric.

2   Circles, crescents and spirals are signatures of her work. Here, circles are randomly overlaid to create spontaneous patterns that cleverly camouflage the repeat.

in there" and the other replied "well, it's just a load of patterns then, we can skip that". At the time I really enjoyed pattern design, but overhearing that comment made me realize that textiles weren't really moving forward in the way that art, design and architecture were.'

Diedrich's first experiments with surface texture incorporated a range of unconventional materials. 'I used rattan in some of my weavings and soaked them in a bath so that they would bend and expand,' she says. 'At times, I also wove with glass. When I was asked to make some upholstery I created a double-weave technique that incorporated pieces of wool to give the surface a richer texture. I knitted and felted textiles to create unconventional surface textures, and made a sculptural, functional textile that looked like a footstool but unrolled flat to create an overnight mattress for a guest.'

A turning point in Diedrich's practice was when she started working with paper. 'I realized that using paper was a quicker way of creating a structured surface than by using fabric.' Diedrich's works received acclaim as artworks, but she decided to pursue a direction in design rather than art. 'I wanted to work in industry rather than craft because I could see more possibilities there,' she explains. 'In the beginning, persuading Swedish manufacturers to produce textiles with holes in them was just as hard as convincing my tutors that it was a new direction. It felt like scaling Mount Everest.'

Diedrich's efforts have been worth the climb, because her professional journey has taken her to the top. She has created printed textiles and laser-cut designs for Kvadrat Sanden, who manufacture her ASAP, HIT, AHIT and EDT designs. IKEA commissioned Diedrich to design the Anno Fin, Anno Ljuv and Anno Skön series of textile panels. In Italy, Rotaliana produce Diedrich's BPL pendant lamp, and a Japanese manufacturer has commissioned a collection of printed fabrics and a graphic wallpaper range. Always keen to map out new terrain, Diedrich has her sights set on exploring the potentials of phototonic textiles. 'I want to make fabrics that light up, but I want to develop a technique that makes that possible without using diodes.' Judging by the rest of Diedrich's pioneering designs, her work with illuminating textiles promises to shed new light on the bright potentials that textiles have ahead of them.

2

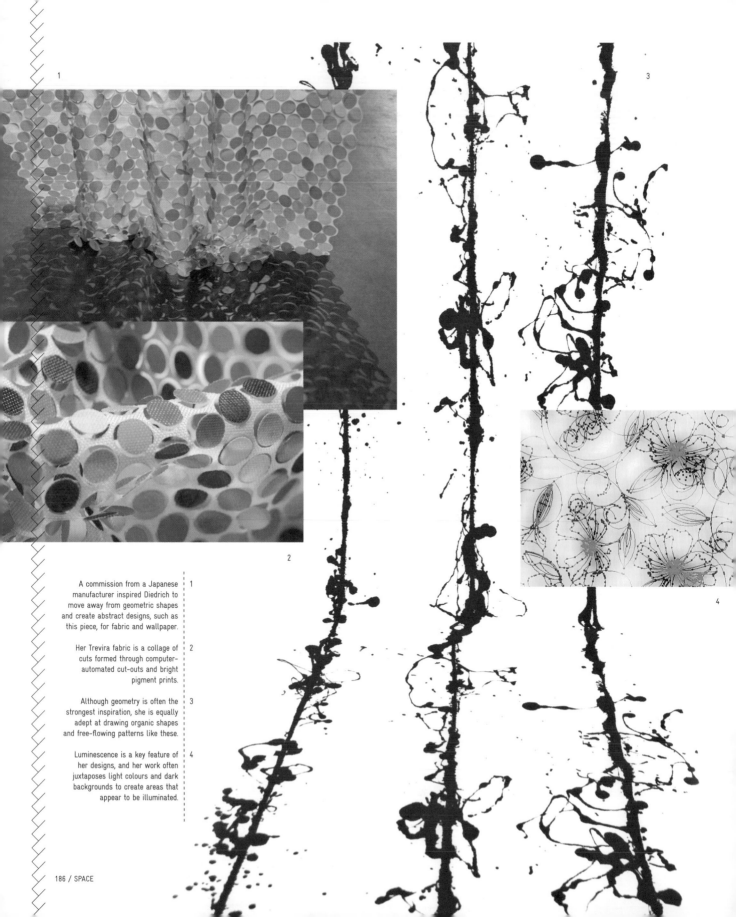

1 A commission from a Japanese manufacturer inspired Diedrich to move away from geometric shapes and create abstract designs, such as this piece, for fabric and wallpaper.

2 Her Trevira fabric is a collage of cuts formed through computer-automated cut-outs and bright pigment prints.

3 Although geometry is often the strongest inspiration, she is equally adept at drawing organic shapes and free-flowing patterns like these.

4 Luminescence is a key feature of her designs, and her work often juxtaposes light colours and dark backgrounds to create areas that appear to be illuminated.

5   Diedrich uses a heat process to create this richly textured bubble effect in sheer textiles. Here, the fabric is shown in anthracite and white.

6   Since Nordic interiors are often decorated with white and light, Scandinavian designers tend to produce light-coloured fabrics. Diedrich likes to counteract pale decor with textiles whose powerful patterns hold their own in the interior.

5

6

4

3

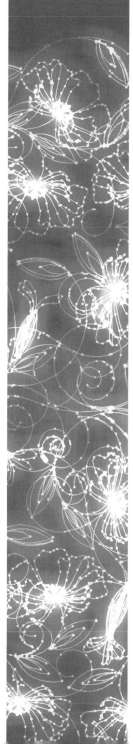

1 Diedrich's BPL pendant lamp
   was designed in Sweden but is
   manufactured today by Italian
   producer Rotaliana.

2 This swatch of her EDT fabric
   reveals how subtle shading and
   reversing the colourways can make
   the repeat less easy to identify.

3 Diedrich is developing illuminating
   textiles that rely on photovoltaic
   pigments and thermocromatic dyes
   rather than optic fibres and LEDs.

4 She uses lasers to create circular
   shapes and spiralling patterns, or
   perforates fabrics with small holes
   to make them semi-transparent.

5 Diedrich has designed an extensive
   range of wall-hangings, pendant
   lamps and minimalist room
   dividers, produced in synthetic
   fabrics and processed materials.

5

1-3 & 5 Much of Diedrich's early work was characterized by the radical cut-outs in her textiles, and her recent works continue to subtract negative spaces. Methods such as laser cutting enable her to eliminate some of the fibres of the fabrics, or to cut motifs directly into the textile's structure.

2

1

3

4   Experimenting with paper inspired Diedrich to create structured surfaces rather than embellish the surface with patterns. It took her several years to convince the textile industry that fabrics with 'holes' in them would attract design-savvy customers, and today even mainstream manufacturers are producing her designs, such as this Anno Ljuv cotton/polyester blend for IKEA.

4

5

HELENA HIETANEN

From her base in Helsinki, the sculptor Helena Hietanen sky-rocketed to worldwide fame when she began creating her spectacular Technolace wall hangings. Fabricated from strands of optic fibres, her works combine handicraft traditions and cutting-edge fibre-optic technology to create textiles that transmit light. Formerly a fibre-artist who explored materials such as rubber strands and human hair, today Hietanen's work pioneers methods of integrating light sources and fabric, and introduces a range of new possibilities for textile design.

Hietanen discovered fibre-optics at a trade fair and, out of curiousity, decided to see if it would be possible to crochet them like yarn. It didn't work, but Hietanen found other ways of using the material. 'One experiment led to another and I found a way to make the optic fibre illuminate along the whole length, not only just from the end point,' Hietanen explains. 'Then I discovered how to adapt it to create traditional lace patterns by combining traditional hand craftsmanship with today's technology, which is what I had wanted to do all along.'

As Hietanen created fibre-optic fabrics she also became adept at handling the material in other ways. She started combining natural light with artificial lighting and even created architectural structures, such as the light wall at the Nobel Museum in Stockholm. 'Working with architects led to a commission for LED lights installed in the façade of a seven-floor apartment building in Helsinki,' she says. 'The LED lighting will be linked to sensors and to a computer interface that measures the movement of the occupants. As people approach the building, LEDs in the walkways and handrails will begin to glow, then intensify in the areas where they detect movement.'

It is easy to see how Hietanen's textile practice engages with art, design, technology and architecture but, surprisingly, she reveals that her work has a sustainable dimension too. 'LEDs consume much less energy than conventional lighting,' she explains. 'Cold temperatures cause a reaction that makes them even brighter without using more electricity. So using LEDs in the cold, dark winter season in Finland means you can have brighter lighting yet consume much less energy.'

Although much of Hietanen's work has centred around fibre optics, she is always on the lookout for other materials that will react with light in a dramatic way. 'I'm attracted to surfaces that reflect natural light or technical materials that produce artificial light,' she says. 'The materials I like the most are silicon crystals, the tiny reflective beads used in highway paints, LED lighting, metals with polished surfaces and pre-woven metal mesh. I like coatings such as transparent silicon rubber and gloss paint. At one time my work revolved around fibres, but now my focus is on light itself.'

1   Helena Hietanen's fibre-optic textiles are a mesmerizing mesh
of illuminated cables twisted and bundled into loops and scrolls.
The cable ends form brilliant points of light that brighten and soften
as they grow in intensity and then fade out again. The effect is that
of an ethereal textile shaped by the patterns and rhythms of light
that pass through it.

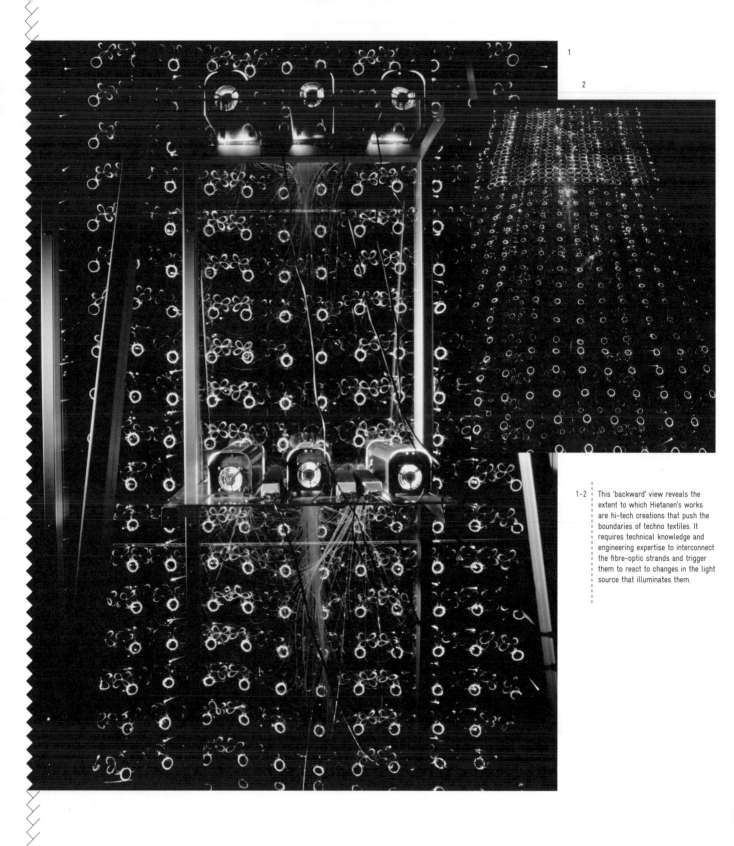

1-2 This 'backward' view reveals the extent to which Hietanen's works are hi-tech creations that push the boundaries of techno textiles. It requires technical knowledge and engineering expertise to interconnect the fibre-optic strands and trigger them to react to changes in the light source that illuminates them.

3-4 These detail shots are from Hietanen's Technolace light sculpture in Paris, where the textile was placed inside a custom-built glass and aluminium cube positioned at the end of the Avenue des Champs-Élysées near the Place de la Concorde. The sculpture was located near l´Obelisque, La Tour Eiffel and l´Arc de Triomphe, perhaps the first time a contemporary textile featured among the great landmarks of the city.

3

4

HIL
DRIESSEN _____

Hil Driessen was born in the Netherlands, where her multi-faceted approach is pioneering new possibilities for textile design. Like many other Dutch designers, Driessen imbues her work with wit, irreverence and experimentation. But unique to Driessen's style is her distinctive vision for material innovation, and her ability to bridge spatial – and perhaps visual – extremes.

Outside the Netherlands, Driessen's work is most easily found in the form of textile prints used as furniture upholstery, like when Konstantin Grcic upholstered his Chaos chair with Reef, one of Driessen's jacquard fabrics. But back home, Driessen, who works collaboratively with Toon van Deijne in the practice they call Driessen + van Deijne, is probably known best for the fibre-based products she has designed and the high-profile architectural commissions she has undertaken. 'From the beginning of my career, architects have used my work for acoustic applications, or just added them as decoration,' Driessen says. 'When I was commissioned to work on an interior at the university of Utrecht, it gave me an opportunity to produce work on a much larger scale than before. And since it was a historical interior, it was the perfect chance to explore Baroque-style trompe l'oeil, which has long been a staple charm in the designer's bag of tricks.'

Driessen was commissioned to produce wall-mounted fabrics for the nineteenth-century period rooms owned by the university. The preservationists had concluded that the original wallpaper from 1859 had deteriorated too far to be restored, yet decided to preserve the decorative paint finishes on the woodwork and cornices. 'It was important to preserve them,' Driessen explains, 'but looking at them doesn't quite transport you to another place. So I knew that the wall textiles would have to do exactly that.'

And they did. Driessen folded and stitched a sheet of vinyl to create the silhouette of an attenuated tree. She then photographed the stitched vinyl in the shadow of a real tree, and used digital technology to manipulate the resulting photograph even further. Driessen printed the shadowy silhouettes onto Trevira CS fabric, and mounted this onto the walls where the original wallpaper had once hung. 'The digitally-printed fabric had visual depth and created a surprisingly tactile surface,' Driessen says. 'People wondered if it was a real landscape or a futuristic image. I saw people stretch out their hand to feel the

texture of the knotted bark, then look again in wonder, realizing they'd been duped. I love to play with illusions.'

Although she may be a master of illusions, Driessen's work is firmly rooted in the material world. Projects featuring glass, metal and ceramics have married soft textile forms to some of the hardest substrates around. 'As a textile designer, the challenge of working with ceramics was a lifetime experience,' Driessen says. 'I was given a residency at the European Ceramic Work Centre here in the Netherlands. Through the help of the technical staff, I was able to develop the process that created my Whitewear products. I dipped pieces of crocheted cotton into liquid porcelain and fired them in the kiln. The cotton burned away, but left its imprint behind.' The objects that resulted were photographed and manipulated digitally using computer software, then printed onto cotton. 'I love the idea of one medium leaving its mark on another,' she says.

Fascinated by processes, Driessen is motivated by the drive to effect transformations. 'Just by padding, stitching, cutting, folding or printing, I can reinvent cheap-looking materials such as imitation leather and rubber as sculptural textiles,' she says. 'But at the same time, it is important to me to stay in touch with technology and collaborate with the industry to develop new materials. I teamed up with Toon van Deijne on a project for DSM Dyneema. It was a supreme opportunity to undertake experiments with what is regarded as the world's strongest fibre. We worked together with DSM Dyneema's technical staff, exploring both hi- and lo-tech processes. While we learned about new technology from them, they said they benefited from our bold and original approach.'

1 Hil Driessen imbues her work with wit and irreverence. These textile swatches, sourced for an interior design project carried out with Toon van Deijne, reminded Driessen of a green landscape; the perfect habitat for a plastic bear.

The Witsen damask design is a 3-4
collage of digital prints photographed
and printed on cotton/viscose
fabric. Driessen used photographs
of Baroque-inspired objects to
create the motif, which renders the
impression of visual depth.

1

2

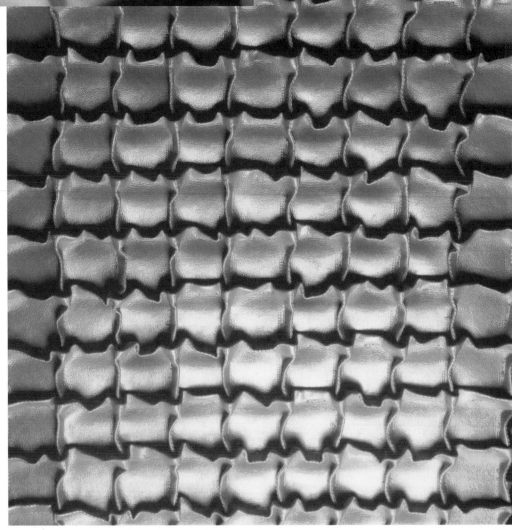

Driessen creates digitally-printed 1-2
motifs by manipulating photographs.
Rather than photographing existing
objects, she creates her own still
life by bringing together objects with
unique textures. Her Geel quilted
cotton fabric features a digital
pattern inspired by the façades
of skyscrapers.

3

4

1   Driessen created this maquette for
    'The Porcelain Cabinet' exhibition held
    in Tillburg in 2003.

2&4 The Reef jacquard fabric was
    designed using CAD images of her
    fibre and ceramic bowls. The motif
    was chosen by Konstantin Grcic
    as upholstery for his Chaos chair
    designed in 2005.

3   This installation was staged to
    create a hyper-realistic universe
    of textile textures. Driessen used
    digital imaging techniques to create
    the motif which she then printed
    on velvet, wove into damask and
    reproduced in a tufted carpet. The
    resulting environment offered a
    sensory experience, which was both
    abstract and narrative, as well
    as futuristic and historical.

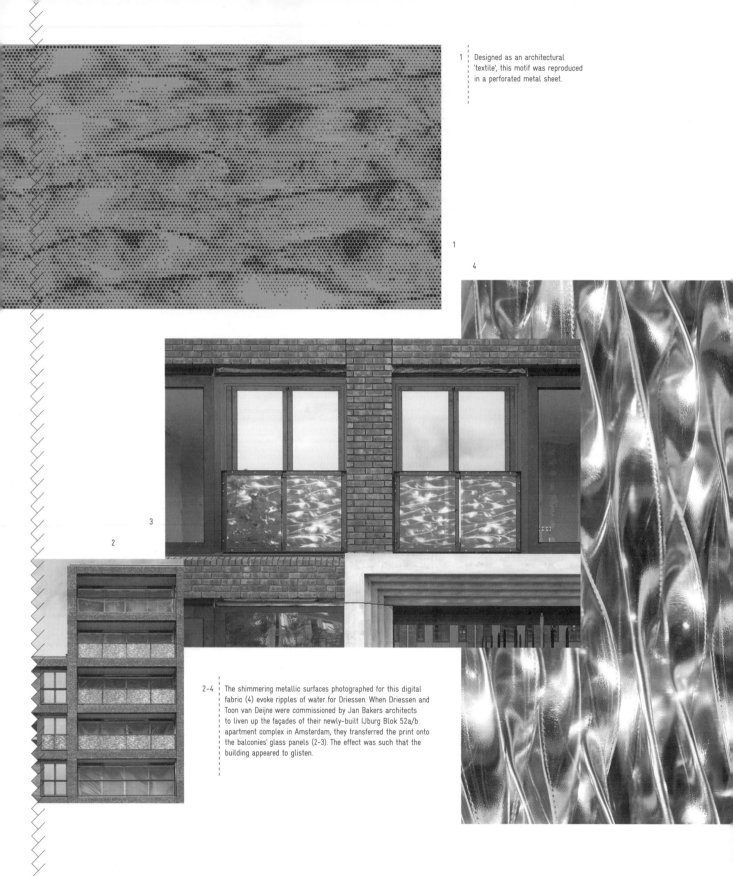

1 Designed as an architectural
   'textile', this motif was reproduced
   in a perforated metal sheet.

1

4

3

2

2–4 The shimmering metallic surfaces photographed for this digital
     fabric (4) evoke ripples of water for Driessen. When Driessen and
     Toon van Deijne were commissioned by Jan Bakers architects
     to liven up the façades of their newly-built IJburg Blok 52a/b
     apartment complex in Amsterdam, they transferred the print onto
     the balconies' glass panels (2–3). The effect was such that the
     building appeared to glisten.

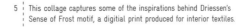

5   This collage captures some of the inspirations behind Driessen's Sense of Frost motif, a digitial print produced for interior textiles.

6   The thin layer of crystals created by winter frost inspired her to photograph similar patterns. These frosty cobbles render a vision of a cold autumn morning on a city street.

7   Driessen's Sense of Frost pattern is presented here in an artistic guise, framed and mounted on the wall like a work of art.

5

6

7

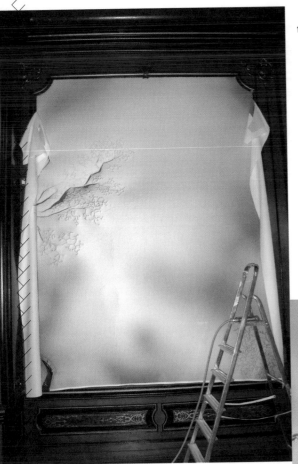

1

2

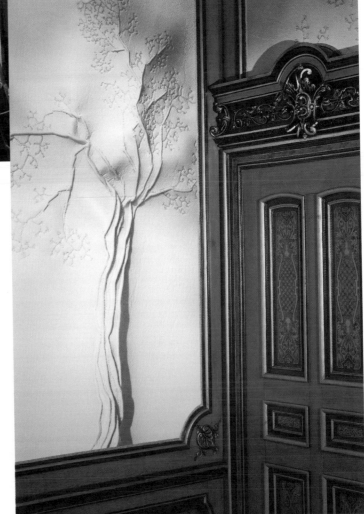

3

Driessen's designs for the renovated 1–4
period rooms at the University of
Utrecht were inspired by Baroque
interiors, where walls held visions
of imaginary landscapes or the
impression of fake windows. Such
historical sensibilities were an
important part of the project, since
the original decorative paintwork on
the interior moulding and woodwork
were required to be left intact.

4

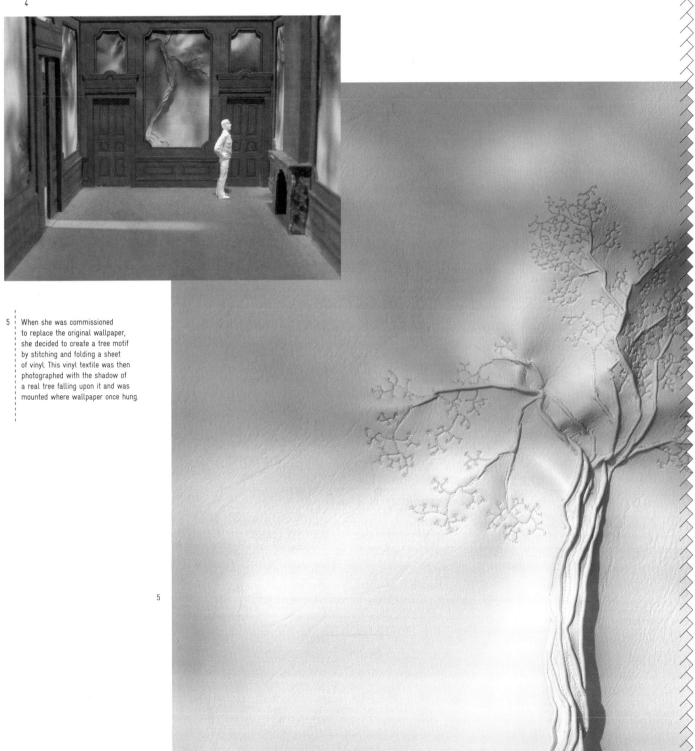

5 When she was commissioned
to replace the original wallpaper,
she decided to create a tree motif
by stitching and folding a sheet
of vinyl. This vinyl textile was then
photographed with the shadow of
a real tree falling upon it and was
mounted where wallpaper once hung.

5

HSIAO-CHI TSAI

Funky, fun or forward thinking? Such words are often attached to works by Taiwanese textile designer Hsiao-Chi Tsai. Finding ways to describe her approach is sometimes difficult, because many of her works straddle the divide between surface design and three-dimensional structures, or move between playful expressions and ground-breaking innovation.

Tsai studied textile design at the Royal College of Art in London, where she discovered her talent for creating large-scale installations. 'My work was always very different from what people expected from textile design,' Tsai explains, 'and that's probably why I received commissions from the Royal Botanic Gardens, Kew, and the Queen Elizabeth Hall at the South Bank Centre.' Shortly after she graduated, Tsai was approached by Harvey Nichols department store and asked to create a continuous chain of Christmas ornaments that would link the upper levels of their 40-metre- (130-foot-) long display windows. 'It was a fantastic opportunity,' Tsai says, 'but after meeting me they decided to offer me a bigger, better project. I designed all of their windows for the Spring of 2007, which was on display throughout February and March.' Tsai decided to collaborate with Kimiya Yoshikawa, a sculptor, to give her two-dimensional ideas three-dimensional form. 'I combined his knowledge of three-dimensional construction with my "magical balloon" theme, and together we created seven individual large-scale sculptures that we called Futuristic Flowers.' The installations that resulted appeared to be layered tableaux of three-dimensional textile motifs and abstract repeats that brought to mind the fictitious world of Dr Seuss. The installations evoked real worlds painted in vivid colours and surreal silhouettes, generating a hallucinatory rush of visual delight.

'It's important to me to create work that is more than two-dimensional,' Tsai explains, 'and to provide different aesthetics and appearances to be seen by viewers from every angle. The structure and texture of my work plays an essential role in giving volume, depth and space to forms that would otherwise remain two-dimensional. The role of structural form in my work enables the textile to become multi-layered by light and shadows and come to life in three-dimensional space.'

Textile innovation is an important part of Tsai's work as she looks for rigid materials that will allow her to 'weave' three-dimensional forms. 'I am constantly looking for new materials to work with,' she says. 'The formable, non-textile materials I use range from foam and plastic to sheet metal and ceramics.

The fabrics I like to work with are Lycra®, felt and polyester. I often laminate materials like plastic and Lycra® together to create a double-sided effect, then cut and mould them into three-dimensional organic forms.'

Tsai's ability to work in a three-dimensional way has inspired her to create products crafted from textiles as well as other materials. 'I want to see how my installation-art ethos can be simplified and still make use of elements such as form, light and shadow to create high-end interior products,' she says. 'I still see textile design as one of the most important ways to visually enhance almost everything in our everyday life, from what we wear to what we use and live with. The future applications of textiles are enormous because textile-based sensibilities will continue to grow and expand in product design, architecture and beyond. Eventually, all functional things will be made with a textile aesthetic.'

1 | Hsiao-Chi Tsai uses a unique three-dimensional foam-cutting technique to create densely-textured plant-like structures and intricate large-scale floral shapes. Her chrysanthemum motif is shown here.

2 | Rainbow Creature is a colourful hanging textile that resembles a three-dimensional kaleidescope.

3 | Tsai's Drop of Light lighting design uses mirrors to reflect and diffuse the light.

3

2

3

1   This installation for the Royal Botanic Gardens, Kew, in London
    mimics trailing vines and blossoming flowers. The textile was
    displayed among live species of exotic plants, where it looked
    very much at home.

2-3   Entitled Corner Explosion, this mirrorscape reflects Tsai's
      sculpture-like floral textile and amplifys it into infinity.
      Many of her works straddle the divide between surface
      design and three-dimensional structures.

1

2

1-3 These site-specific installations were
commissioned by Harvey Nichols
department store in London. Called
Futuristic Flowers, the installations
were made for seven window
displays and exhibited during
London Fashion Week in Spring
2007. Tsai teamed up with Japanese
sculptor Kimiya Yoshikawa to scale
her designs into larger-than-life
proportions. She also designed small-
scale pieces for the mannequins to
wear as fashion accessories.

3

4

5

4 | Tsai's work relies on volume, depth and space to structure forms that would otherwise remain two-dimensional. The textile structures that result are often multi-layered, and use light and shadow to enhance their visual impact.

5 | She created this maquette to render a three-dimensional image of a proposed airport installation. The work was intended to create an artifical landscape of surreal flowers and plant forms.

Entitled simply Purple and Gold
Leaves, this hanging textile features
leafy textures and leaf-like cut-outs.
Although crafted from a single piece,
it has the appearance of a more
complex layered tableaux.

1

1

2

3

2-3 Rigid materials are a source of fascination for Tsai, who looks for strong and sturdy forms that will allow her to create three-dimensional shapes. Non-textile materials, such as thick plastic, sheet metal and ceramics have enabled her to recreate fabric motifs three-dimensionally. Her porcelain Coralight design is a colourful luminescent tube illuminated from within.

Tsai's Wisteria hanging textile, is
seen in the artist's studio (1) and
in situ at the 'Poetry International'
festival held at the South Bank
Centre in 2006 (2). The hangings
were commissioned for the festival's
stage design.

1–2

3

4

3-4 | Tsai describes her Wonderland
collection as 'couture fashion
jewellery pieces'. These accessories
are so striking they may even
upstage the garments they are
intended to enhance.

JOHAN CARPNER

The beauty of Johan Carpner's work lies in the way it moves. Not movement as in coaxing three-dimensional depth out of a flat surface, but movement in terms of how easily his style flows between the intense lucidity of his graphic designs and the haunting expressiveness of his textiles.

After working for almost a decade as a graphic designer, Carpner peeled graphic symbols off the printed page and gave them new life as patterns and motifs. Finally free of fonts, templates and T-squares, he began to express himself in free-flowing organic lines and leafy abstractions. Drawn to serpentine outlines and razor-sharp cut-outs, his textile prints for Swedish luxury retailer Svenskt Tenn stopped onlookers in their tracks. In Winter Oak, which Svenskt Tenn produced in 2004, the harsh reality of the Nordic winter was recreated in a tangle of bare tree branches depicted solemnly against the stark January sky. 'I've always been fascinated by how people try to tame nature despite knowing they'll never actually succeed,' Carpner says. 'It's the wildness in nature that gives it its beauty. I like capturing the inexpressible and the untameable, because to me, that's realism, and that's what tests the boundaries of pattern drawing. I like finding order in chaos, for example, by exploring how something chaotic, like the jumble of tree branches in this case, can be given a gestalt as they grow in nature and not as how they are cultivated by man. Contrasts are also important to me, because they can create an essential edge. Without that, patterns just become decorative and sweet, and that's not what my work is about.'

In Carpner's capable hands, pattern design is treated robustly and imbued with masculine sensibilities. Given that textile design has traditionally been characterized by a feminine aesthetic, Carpner's approach is as directional as it is refreshing. 'Most textile designers begin with an education in textile design and probably continue to repeat what they learned as their career goes on,' Carpner explains. 'Coming from a graphic design background, my references lie more in poster design and graphic art, which is probably what you're describing as a masculine expression. And that's probably why my work is so tightly focused on form rather than on decoration.'

1-2   Johan Carpner finds beauty in nature wherever he looks. Weeds and spring flowers growing by the kerbside inspired this design called Vägren, shown here in horizontal repeats. He believes that capturing the spontaneous aspects of nature tests the boundaries of pattern-drawing, but he finds it satisfying to create order out of chaos.

3   Wild roses are likely to be found in forest glades and overgrown gardens, but Carpner's Wild Rose motif brings them into the interior.

Carpner took paternity leave when his children were born, and during the year-long breaks he found that he wanted to express himself in three-dimensional forms. 'I realized that I'm an inventive person, someone who likes to construct things and solve three-dimensional problems,' Carpner says. 'That's when I became interested in textiles and product design, because they gave me the chance to design things like lamps, carpets and furniture. I wouldn't say that I'll ever leave graphic design altogether; right now, I'm enjoying balancing the two.'

Coming into an aspect of interior design as an outsider, at a time when more and more Swedes were becoming interested in home decoration, enabled Carpner to view the phenomenon with fresh eyes. 'I noticed that the boom was changing what interior design means today,' Carpner says. 'It's not about having good taste or a single style anymore, but combining many different styles in a way that hasn't happened earlier. These days, you can draw a lot of parallels between buying things for the home and shopping for clothes, and I think that textiles have probably made the home fashionable again.'

2

3

2

3

4

1-3 : The view of the sky through a canopy
of birch branches overhead was
the inspiration for Carpner's Glänta
(Forest Glade) motif. Adapted for this
pendant lamp, the motif creates the
impression of sunlight shining through
the trees.

4 : His Utsikt (View) print suggests the
view of a vine viewed through a
window. Framed and wall-mounted,
the print provides a uniquely naturalistic focal point for this interior.

Vägren (page 216) is a versatile motif
that can be appreciated from several
perspectives. Here, printed in a dark
colourway, the pattern is presented in
vertical direction.

1–2

Carpner's Wild Rose motif (page 217).

3

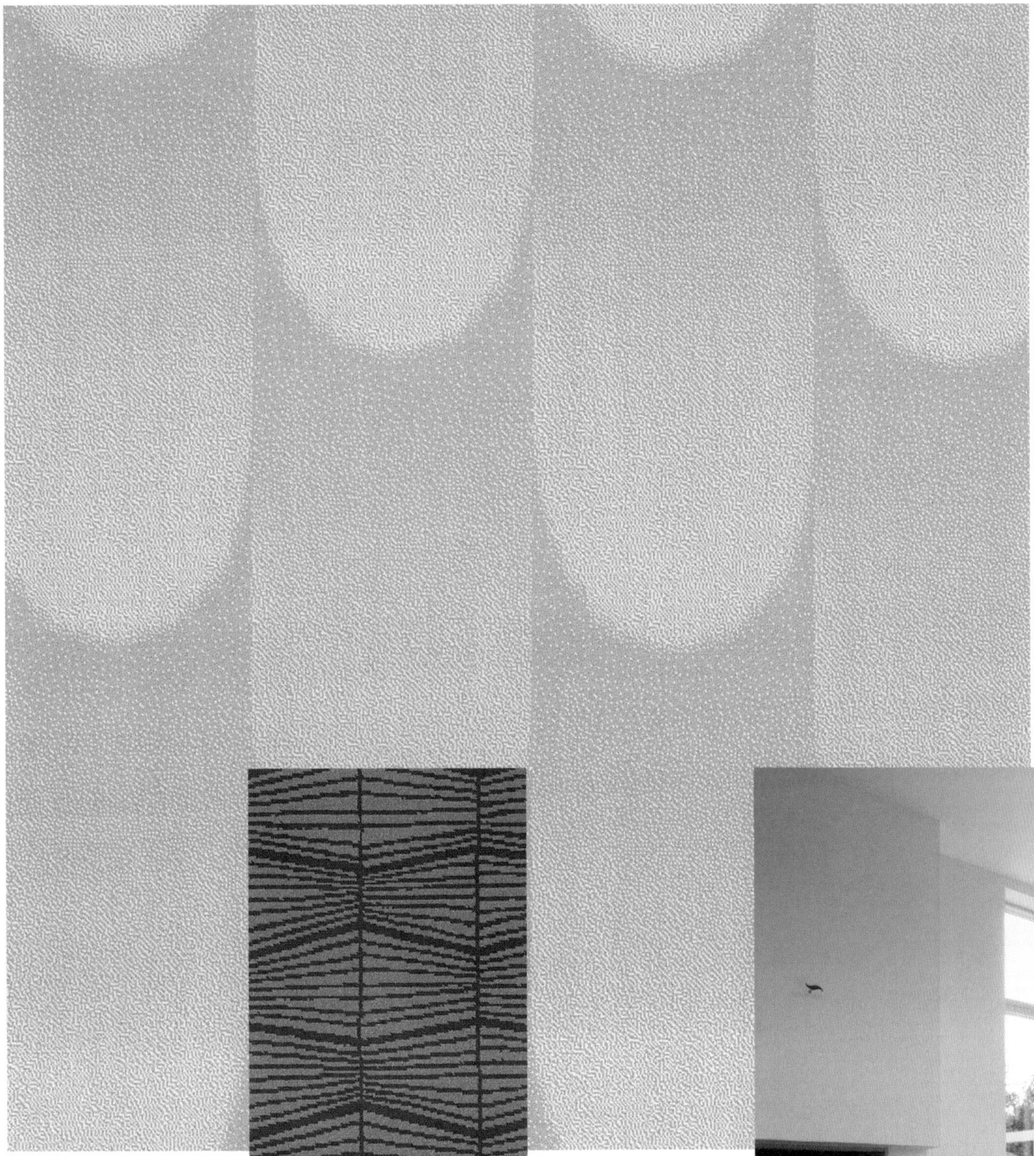

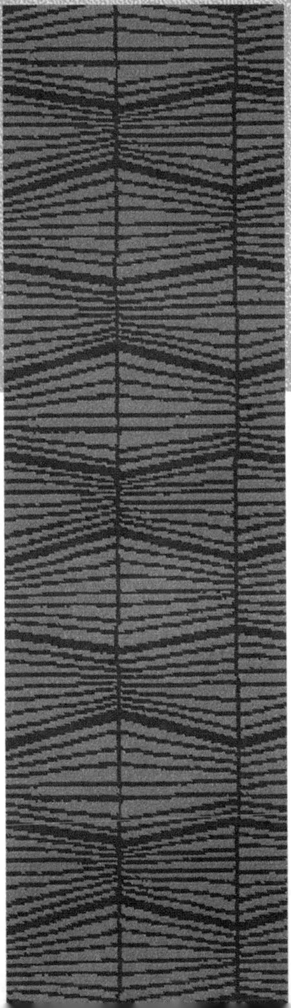

1   Carpner's Winter Oak fabric,
    designed and produced in 2004,
    captures the stark beauty of the
    Nordic winter in this tangle of bare
    tree branches depicted solemnly
    against a stark snow-filled sky.

2&4 As its name suggests, Storm
    captures a foreboding canopy of
    cumulus clouds rolling in, moments
    before the heavens open. Here,
    Carpner has transformed the
    fluffy, free-flowing outlines of
    cloud formations into a graphic,
    geometric repeat.

3   The designer's graphic approach to
    motifs means that they can easily
    peel off the printed page and onto
    the surfaces of tufted carpets.
    Swedish manufacturer Kasthall
    commissioned designs for several
    carpets, such as the vibrant Brygga
    motif, shown here.

2

3

4

KATE
GOLDSWORTHY

British designer Kate Goldsworthy is something out of the ordinary, not only because she has passion for sustainable design, but also because she venerates the materials that most textile designers shy away from. 'The materials I use are, in themselves, completely unremarkable,' smiles Goldsworthy. 'In fact, it is actually their extreme "ordinariness" that I find so appealing. I work with non-woven polyesters and the robust felts used to make carpet underlay, insulation, household textiles, medical bandaging and geo-textiles. These materials are the unseen "work-horses" of the textile world. Because they are rarely used as outward-facing materials, they are almost always hidden from view.'

Textiles of this type are manufactured in large volumes, providing a reliable secondary resource for industrial recycling. Yet, few manufacturers have realized that these secondary fabrics can easily be reinvented as sustainable textiles. 'Whether you realize it or not, these materials are a precious resource, and I treat them that way,' she says. 'By revealing their hidden beauty, I can elevate them to a higher status and make them more desirable to consumers.'

The processes Goldsworthy pioneers always take waste as their starting point, and efficiently convert it into source material. But since she is an aesthete, her methods transform trash into treasure; she is committed to making the finished product look good. 'The processes I'm developing are inspired by the traditions of lace making, appliqué and marquetry, but also the hi-tech polymer recycling technologies that use experimental surface treatments to "upgrade" samples of mixed-fibre waste,' she explains. Goldsworthy resurfaces mixed-fibre felt by layering reclaimed non-woven materials on its outer surface. The finish it yields gives the surface a uniquely structured texture that looks as good – if not better – than many bonded fabrics. 'New technologies make resurfacing a viable and sustainable method of producing "up-cycled" textile products,' she says.

Goldsworthy's design processes are rooted in the 'cradle to cradle' theory espoused by Michael Braungart and William McDonough in their book of the same name. 'Much of my work explores the "mono-materiality" advocated in *Cradle to Cradle*, with the intention that products can be recycled through multiple life-cycles,' she explains. 'Technology is beginning to provide alternative

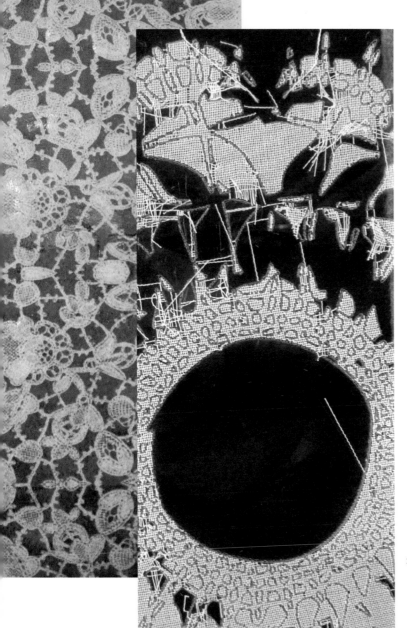

1   Kate Goldsworthy explores the
    potentials of using existing
    recycling and finishing technology
    to re-process synthetic fabric. This
    re-surfaced textile is produced for
    use within window treatments.

2   She is pioneering new textile
    construction methods, finishing
    and cutting techniques. Her
    work also explores decorative
    applications for polymer
    engineering by adapting them
    for recycled textiles.

answers and systems, especially in the field of recycling. For example, the Eco-Circle process that re-polymerizes 100% polyester fabrics into virgin-quality polyester fibre is overcoming some of the problems associated with mechanical textile recycling, because it results in better fibre quality.'

Rather than using a sewing machine or print table, Goldsworthy uses emerging laser technology, plastic-processing methods and heat-bonding tools. When she used these processes to layer sequin-like recycled polyester discs in her MultiSheer pieces – lampshades and interior textiles – she produced a remarkable three-dimensional effect. 'I wanted the fabrics' decorative elements to be removable, updatable and recyclable,' she says, 'so that their replaceability would be an essential quality of the design.' Goldsworthy mainly works with thermoplastic materials such as polyester, which she says represent over 50% of global fibre production today. 'Thermoplastics have very specific properties that yield to heat by melting, expanding and contracting, and this can be used to form them in a way which isn't possible with natural fibres.'

Despite her commitment to reclaiming synthetic wastes, natural fibres also play a central role in Goldsworthy's work when they feature in blended-fibre materials. 'Natural fibres follow the laws of nature,' she says. 'They are grown, processed and can biodegrade to fuel future growth as part of an agricultural cycle. Synthetic materials are not part of this cycle and need to be processed separately.' Her resurfaced materials address this problem, because they can be mechanically recycled through further life-cycles when needed.

Although Goldsworthy describes today's textile industry as a world where materials have been devalued virtually to the point of disposability, she is optimistic about the way forward. 'I am really encouraged by the discussion emerging around the new luxury created through eco-design,' she says. 'I would love to think that the future holds a culture of rediscovered delight in the value of recycled resources, and a renewed respect for the time and care it takes to produce beautiful textiles.'

2

1&3 Goldsworthy's resurfaced materials employ both hand-crafted and digital techniques to produce multi-media textiles for interior design applications.

2 Her work reveals the process of construction and the materials used. Her research highlights the stories behind everyday products, exposing how they're made, the materials used, energy consumed and distances they travelled, in an innovative and accessible exhibition that shows how design can make a difference.

4–5 | The beauty of Goldsworthy's resurfaced designs has shifted many misconceptions surrounding recycling, revealing that worn out materials can be reinvented and improved. Her work is inspired by light, transparency and movement, resulting in designs that are multi-layered, sheer and dynamic.

4

5

1

3

2

1&4 Shown in red and white respectively, these interior textile panels are made from recycled PET plastic decorated with laser etched detail The red version is one of Goldsworthy's multi-sheer window treatments.

2-3 Displayed in the windows of
the Royal Festival Hall, London,
Goldsworthy's multi-sheer panels
create an engaging interface
between inside and outside spaces.
Ultimately they aim to develop
innovative, yet commercially viable,
designs that will respond to those
'material limitations' in order to
suggest creative solutions for the
future recycling of thermoplastic
materials.

5   A multi-sheer design, shown here
in anthracite and black.

1   Not only is this textile (page 227)
made from recycled material, it has
been crafted in such a way that it
can also be recycled when no longer
in use.

2   Goldsworthy's thermoplastic
fabrics combine new engineering
and finishing technology currently
emerging in both textiles and
plastics fields. Textiles like these
are seen as being in an 'interim'
state; that is, produced from
recycled materials and capable
of being 'upcycled' into a new
form at the end of their life span.

3   The designer's techniques can
create fashion fabrics as well
as interior textiles.

4   Her work has set a new standard
for environmentally-friendly interior
fabrics and has inspired a new
generation of recyclable textiles.

6

5-7 Goldsworthy's 'well-fashioned' clothing series explores ways in which fashion and textiles are a reflection of changing attitudes about design and consumption. Her ethos recalls the philosophy underpinning the British Arts and Crafts movement, which, even in the late nineteenth century, brought together designers seeking methods of unifying technology and the creative process.

7

LOOP

With their edgy textures, technological interfaces and interactive surfaces, the structures created by Loop are some of the most visionary expressions of textiles today. From their studio in London's East End, the design duo of British-born Royal College of Art textiles graduate Rachel Wingfield and Austrian artist Mathias Gmachl, join an emerging generation of environmentally-aware designers. Loop pioneer a new way of thinking about textiles; as they bridge the gap between the built environments of man and the leafy structures of nature, they create boldly interactive designs that grow, glow, respond and even biodegrade.

'Our starting point is often a growing form, usually a plant, but other types of biological structures are also interesting to us,' Wingfield explains. 'Plants fascinate us because they use energy so efficiently. When you consider the structures they create when they grow, you can imagine that plants probably provided the inspiration for early weaving techniques. Just look at how vines spin, weave and knot themselves around other structures. And as they grow, they establish stable networks and use energy efficiently.'

Loop's organic oeuvre is often driven by their fascination with ecosystems, which they aim to recreate biomimetically as they design textile-based responsive environments. 'Merging bio-systems with textile techniques can improve our material world in many ways,' Wingfield explains. 'The place where man-made materials meet natural systems is not primarily in biotech, but in architecture. Textiles are often the backbone of most architectural environments, and if you scale textiles up to architectural proportions and equip them with biomimetic sensors, you can create a responsive environment.'

Wingfield cites Cambridge scientist John Walker – a recent Nobel Laureate – as a source of inspiration. Walker describes living cells as 'molecular machines' due to the energy released by individual cells. 'The relationship between energy and structure that John Walker researches scientifically is something that we explore in both textiles and wider design practices. If Mathias and I can recreate a molecular structure in a dynamic textile and scale it up to architectural proportions, we can create a sustainable environment.'

1   This luminescent motif is from Loop's Digital Dawn reactive window blind. By using phosphorous printing inks that emit light with electrical manipulation, the blind mimics the process of photosynthesis on a textile surface.

2   Sonumbra was a temporary interactive installation in Sunderland. The installation used an octagonal umbrella structure to map people's movement and record them on its surface. As it did so, a unique environment of light and sound was created.

Loop's vision for future textiles is to conceive them as live membranes formed by living fibres that grow organically and weave whole structures. This idea was pioneered in Loop's BioWall project, a 'woven' three-dimensional structure that can be produced in a wide range of dimensions and configurations. 'We were initially very excited about the prospect of using plant matter to structure and divide space,' Wingfield says. 'We thought about how hedges mark territory outdoors and decided to mimic that in an interior. We originally wanted to create a lace-like partition that plants could mesh with as they grow.'

The basis of the BioWall structure is fibrous, and its construction mimics a textile structure. Fibreglass rods are bent into rings and woven into several dodecahedra that are fused together. 'The woven fibres create a balance between the rigidity of sheet material and the flexibility of a textile,' Wingfield explains. 'The structure is based on the principle of self-similarity, enabling it to work from the nano to the macro scale. Structures like it are also found in the formation of bubbles, living cells and water molecules.'

In eco terms, the BioWall is far more sustainable than most interior textiles or building materials. As the growing plants climb a thin, eco-friendly frame, they convert natural substances into plant matter, bypassing manufacturing processes. Compared to a typical production model of growing, harvesting and processing materials to manufacture a textile or a piece of furniture, the sustainable benefits are much higher.

'Mass-produced interior textiles can still be sustainable if they are designed to mimic an eco-system,' Wingfield explains. 'Our design responsive window covering, for example, relies on sensors to synthesize its immediate surroundings and regulate temperature, moisture and energy, and emit light when it detects darkness.' Loop is also pioneering a textile that would harness ambient energy and feed it into a power source. 'Imagine a textile lampshade that can store the energy released by the bulb, then funnel it back into the bulb's power source. It could continually recharge itself.'

Loop's experiments with harnessing natural and artificial light energy led them to electroluminescent printing, a process that integrates the superfine electronic phosphor-coated circuits developed by NASA into fabrics. 'Our Light Sleeper bedding is a programmable duvet and pillowcase that functions as an alarm clock,' Wingfield explains, 'that wakes the sleeper by slowly lighting up, just like dawn breaking in the darkness.' Although Light Sleeper is still in development, a prototype reveals how viable the design is. 'Conventional bedding manufacturers are concerned that there may be some health and safety problems with electronic textiles, so we want to make sure that they're as safe as ordinary bedding before we move forward.'

Light effects and textile technology merged beautifully in Loop's History tablecloth, which illuminates in response to the pressure of objects placed on it. As china and glassware were moved around the table, the impressions they made in the fabric created a visual record of where they had been placed and how long they had sat there. Another illuminating textile, Digital Dawn, is a wall hanging that glows brighter as ambient light levels fall. 'New photovoltaics are forging fresh directions for textiles,' Wingfield says. 'We're focusing on translating some of the electronics created for material science into new textile forms. When decorative textiles store light energy and automatically release it when light levels fade, they become as functional as they are beautiful.'

1   2

3

4

1. The Sonumbra umbrella has an outer surface that can be illuminated at night. Loop acquired the umbrella from German manufacturers MDT-Tex, who had developed its illuminated surface for an advertising campaign.

2. The Digital Dawn window blind (page 232), triggers the foliage motif to appear and disappear as light levels change. The work explores how fabric can maintain an interactive dialogue with its environment.

3. Weather Patterns was a light installation displaying the changing weather patterns outside York Art Gallery. Loop used luminous glass windows with digital sensors to animate them.

4. Entitled Light Sleeper, this bed linen has an integrated silent alarm clock. Simulating dawn, it wakes the sleeper slowly by illumination using electroluminescent technology.

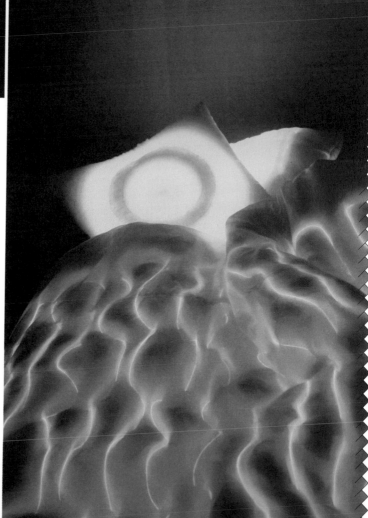

1   Loop have created a modular screening system that uses plant life to divide interior spaces. BioWall was inspired by how hedgerows demarcate outdoor spaces, Loop created a structural unit in which plants could grow in and around.

2   The modular geodesic shapes used in the Wall's construction were inspired by the structures of natural forms such as bubbles and plant cells.

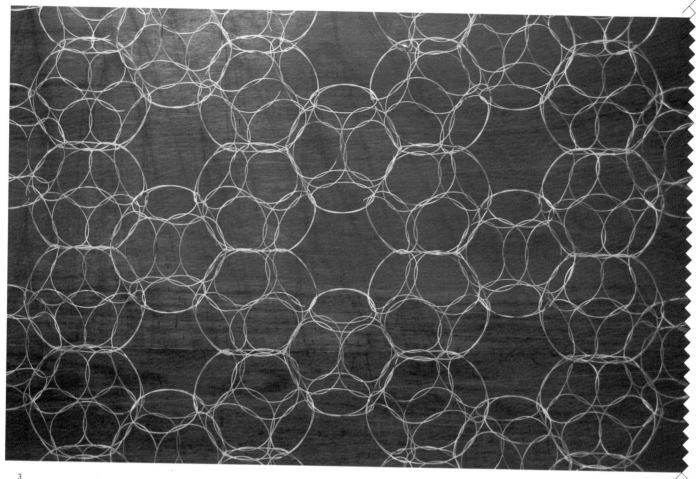

3

3   BioWall's woven construction takes shape through a 'dodecahedron weave' technique Loop developed, that interlocks 1mm (0.04in) thick fibreglass rods. Twelve rods are bent into circles and woven together to make the basic 'building block' component, of which six are then woven into a closed ring pattern.

4   The Wall exemplifies Loop's vision for future textiles. They conceive interior structures as living membranes formed by living fibres that grow organically and weave to form whole structures – even internal walls.

4

MAIJA LOUEKARI

When Maija Louekari won a design competition held by Finnish fabric magnate Marimekko, it was a textile designer's dream come true. A graduate student at the time, Louekari was searching for a way to combine the interior design education she had gained previously with her talent for drawing. 'Textile design really took me by surprise,' she says. 'I became a textile designer by accident, because I got offered a job at Marimekko after I won the competition.'

Since then, Louekari has never looked back. She has consistently produced striking designs characterized by vibrant colour combinations and expressive motifs. Louekari typically depicts the modernist mayhem of the urban centre, as captured in prints such as Hetkiä and Ystävät, or portrays tranquil settings in the natural world, such as Kaiku and Ho-hoi!. 'Cities inspire me with their energy, the people, buildings, events and phenomena,' she says. 'Cities are multi-layered and multi-dimensional; they function as entities but yet come alive through the power of individuals. And they are related to nature too, because they are the "nests" of people.' When it comes to her representations of nature, Louekari regards them to be a continuation of Marimekko's distinctive style. 'Marimekko has always been a portrayer of nature, so I wanted to design my own versions of nature motifs,' she says. 'The purpose of a natural motif is to bring a view of the landscape into a domestic space.'

Although Louekari derives inspiration from observing her surroundings, in some ways she works in isolation, focusing more on channelling the 'Marimekko spirit' rather than following textile trends emerging in other parts of the world. 'Marimekko has such a strong and great history that it seems like a movement in itself. In my work I try to create only my own signature rather than following what's happening elsewhere in the textile industry.'

In addition to cityscapes and representations of nature, Louekari also designs geometric repeats and figurative motifs. Rather than differentiate between them, she tends to regard both expressions as a single abstract style. 'It may be possible to find references to something figurative in the geometric patterns I create,' she explains, 'because one can find points that open up the world of the pattern. Many buyers regard geometric patterns as an easy solution for the interior decoration, and abstract styles give the

viewers the freedom to interpret the design in the way that they want to.'

While she remains committed to the Marimekko ethos and her talent for interpreting her surroundings through textile design, neither is a driving force for Louekari. 'The most important thing is to work with love,' she says. 'It shows if love is present or not. It's wonderful to be able to share something of myself with others through my fabrics. My own work seems a bit like little children being sent out into the wide world.'

1   Finland is renowned for its beautiful coastline and open landscapes. Maija Louekari's Kaiku motif, designed in 2004, is a pastoral design that captures the silence and solitude of the wilderness. 250cm (98in) long, it a floor-to-ceiling tapestry.

2   The Ystävät motif depicts a group of figures with postures to suggest they are a group of strangers.

1 Inspired by the urban landscape,
   the busy street scene, Hetkiä, is an
   antidote to the quiet, rural scenes
   of Louekari's other works.

2 Aarni, designed in 2007, depicts a
   devastating scene. Trees have had
   their limbs sawn off, as if Louekari
   is making a comment on global,
   or local, deforestation.

3 Another section from the Kaiku fabric
   (page 238), which celebrates the
   unspoiled beauty of the natural world.

4 Ho-hoi!, designed in 2004, renders a
   vision of the Finnish coastline, seen
   from beneath a pine tree bowing over
   the water's edge.

3

4

1

2

3

1   In Isosatakieli, Louekari sketches
    out a portrait of a young woman,
    conveyed through colourful birds
    and exotic flowers.

2-3 The Pääsky (Swallow) motif, is an
    intricate assemblage of geometric
    shapes. A colourful design, it
    depicts a snowy hilltop with bright,
    geometric outlines perforated by a
    flock of flying birds.

1–2 A trip to Buenos Aires provided
the inspiration behind Louekari's
La Boca motif.

3–4 Designed in 2006, the Kuiskaaja
motif features sketched outlines
and bold colour swatches.
Its landscape, figures and
mystical owl make it seem
like a contemporary fairy-tale.

1

1 The fractal planes and geometric repeats of Louekari's Vapaapudotus reveal that her work has another dimension beyond figurative works and naturalistic expressions. For her, the more abstract designs are important as they give viewers the freedom to interpret the pattern as they like.

2 Kulkue, designed in 2007, depicts child-like figures marching out together. The motif seems emblematic of how Louekari views her designs, which she describes by saying 'My own work seems a bit like little children being sent out into the wide world.'

3-4 The Kassiopeia motif, 2006, is breathtaking in its use of vivid, bold colours and elaborate details.

2

4

3

NANI
MARQUINA ------------------------

Famous for her unique style and highly individualistic designs, Barcelona-based designer Nani Marquina is to Spanish textiles what Gaudí was to anthropomorphic architecture. She studied industrial design at Barcelona's Massana School of Art and Design and became an interior designer after graduation. Unable to find contemporary textiles that suited her design schemes, Marquina decided to create her own – a move that later inspired her to establish her own textile studio and subsequently open a showroom in Barcelona.

Marquina's speciality is woollen carpets, and her designs take traditional rug design to new tactile heights. She weaves a web of artistic connections as she collaborates with individual designers such as Joaquim Ruiz Millet, Javier Mariscal, Martí Guixé and Diego Fortunato, and design duos such as Ana Mir & Emili Padrós. The vibrant carpets that result reflect the talents of Spain's emerging design scene. International designers, such as Tord Boontje, have also been invited to create carpets that reflect Spanish sensibilities yet appeal to audiences beyond the country's borders. 'Ever since I started my company, I've been commissioning carpets from external designers who normally don't do rugs,' Marquina says. 'Their collaborations introduce concepts that I may not have thought of myself, and feed into the overall creative process in many ways. The guest designers I work with possess a Nani Marquina soul, because they share my love for colour, innovative materials and rich textures.'

Marquina's textured designs are characterized by the striking depth of the materials she uses. Ranging from softly tufted low-pile reliefs to long strands of fluffy wool fibres, her carpets seem ready to embrace the whole body, rather than just cushion the feet. 'Textures are a way of representing the union of two feelings: view and touch,' she explains. 'When we experience a texture, whether in a two-dimensional sketch, on the surface of a stone or when we draw across the sand on a beach, we stretch out our hand to touch it and capture the way it feels. This is the kind of sensation that our rugs create, and that's what makes them attractive. Our rugs invite you to touch them and feel them; people want to stay close to them.'

1

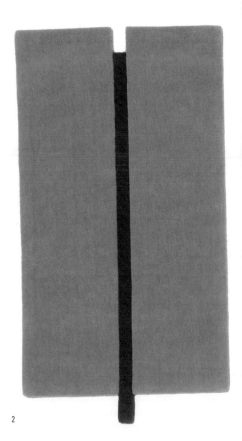

2

3

Many of Marquina's textures are inspired by nature and she readily accepts the challenge of recreating the beauty of the natural world in fibre form. 'There's nothing more perfect than nature,' she says. 'Observing nature inspires me, and gives me the sensibility that I capture in my rugs. You can easily see this in designs such as Roses or Topissimo, carpets that feature die-cut flower forms and moss-like tufted fibres. All of my designs have some kind of essence which belongs to nature's world.' Marquina's commitment to natural wool, cotton fibres and hand-craft production reinforce her links to nature. Although she considered using synthetic materials at one point, Marquina found them to be incompatible with her ethos. 'Artificial fibres and craft production don't really go together,' she explains. 'I prefer using natural and traditional materials, because they are closer to our design concept and our commitment to natural, renewable and recyclable materials and the use of sustainable energy. Our methods of craft production help to maintain and improve natural resources for the use and enjoyment of future generations.'

1   Rounded tufts of woollen fibres are fixed to a cotton base to form
    Nani Marquina's Partida carpet, a design crafted in New Zealand wool.
    The fibres are attached to the base with the aid of a pistol-like device
    that 'fires' them into a latex solution.

2   Her Pull carpet consist of three planes of fabric – each of them pulled
    in a different direction. The carpet has an interesting assymetrical
    shape that easily lends itself to a contemporary interior.

3   The Aros design is painterly in its abstract interpretation of a round
    motif. The carpet recalls the work of Adolf Gottlieb, who depicted the
    outline of the sun boldly against planes of contrasting colour.

1

3

2

1-3 Marquina regularly invites guest designers to contribute to collections, and her Black on White series includes motifs from artists and designers active on the Spanish design scene. Shown here is the winding Limbo designed by Xano Armenter; the Flores motif designed by Sybilla; and, the Estambul motif, a homage to Turkish carpets, by Javier Mariscal.

4

5

6

4-6 The cubic shapes in Marquina's
Cuadros carpet brings pixellated
images to mind, but no pixel
has ever possessed the texture
and tactility of her work. The
pattern repeats are based
on interconnectedness rather
than repetition, where each
complementary form is a unique
shape in itself.

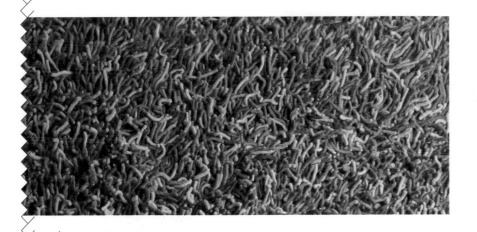

1

2

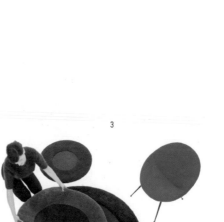

4

3

1　This Seagrass carpet is made for dry land, yet its colours and textures create the sensation of being submerged underwater and lying in a bed of seaweed.

2　Marquina's Dots design bridges textile design with contemporary art. Artists such as Roy Lichtenstein and Damien Hirst have famously used the dot as a motif, and Marquina gives them artistic expression in textile form.

3-5　The Fit series, designed by Oriol Guimerà and Mariana Eidler, is a unique group of tufted carpets that nests together to form a single soft carpet. Taken apart, the components can be interspersed throughout the interior as three single carpets or clustered together.

6   One side of the Floc carpet has an
    unexpected finish with the jagged
    shapes along its edge mimic cuts
    made by pinking shears.

7   The Juliette carpet mimics a
    classical floral motif.

1

2

3

The softly-textured Dolce carpet was designed by Martín Azúa and Gerard Moliné.   1&6

Named Potten, this series of textile containers by Renske Papavoine encases layers of multi-coloured fabrics within a layer of white latex. The forms that result are waterproof and surprisingly pliable.   2-3

4

5

6

4-5 Anyone lucky enough to own one of these beautiful carpets would
readily describe their life as the proverbial 'bed of roses'. Marquina's
stunning Roses carpet caused a sensation when it was launched
at the Salone Internazionale del Mobile in Milan in 2006. Its pile is
comprized of interlocking, petal-shaped pieces of felt wool held in
place by three interconnected warps.

1   Marquina's Nature motif arranges rectalinear planes of soft colours into a mosaic-like motif.

2-3 Whereas most tourists would record their travel experiences in a photo album or travel diary, Marquina decided to capture her experiences in India in a carpet. Entitled Rajasthan, the carpet captures some of the colours and motifs that caught her eye in India.

4   Rangoli is an Indian-inspired motif. Meaning 'wall art', it is a craft practice that decorates surfaces using paint made from fine grains of sand and colourful pigments. Rangoli motifs are commonly seen outside homes in India, especially during the Devali festival.

7

6

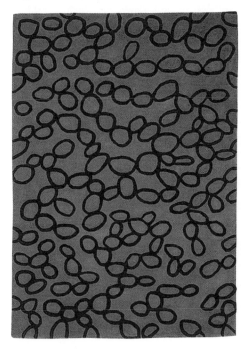

5

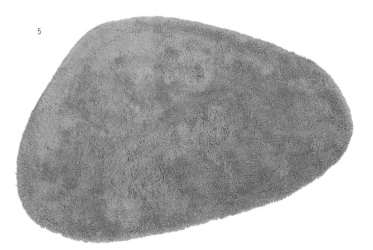

5   The Stone Wool design by Diego
    Fortunato reproduces the outline
    of a smooth rock in a soft carpet.
    Fortunato is an Argentinean designer
    known for his furniture and household
    accessories. His collaboration with
    Marquina began after he moved
    to Barcelona.

6   Marquina sketched egg shapes to
    create the surface motif of her raised
    relief Ovo carpet, made in hand-tufted
    New Zealand wool.

7   One of Marquina's most minimal
    designs, the Zen carpet features a
    simple but effective motif created by
    intersecting lines sketched across a
    contrasting background.

1–2 The Victoria carpet is by Sybilla, the American-born designer who established the Spanish Jocomomola fashion label. In addition to collaborating with Marquina, Sybilla also produces designs for manufacturers such as Alessi.

1

2

3

4

3-5 The richly-textured Topissimo carpet
is characterized by its striking depth.
Its softly-tufted surfaces bring
coloured cotton buds to mind. Its
tufts are created from fluffy wool
fibres that seem ready to embrace
the whole body, rather than just
the feet.

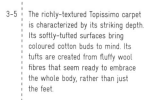

5

2

1

3

The Pisame Mucho designs resemble an ariel view of a landscape. No
matter how abstract her nature references may seem, Marquina says
that every one of her carpets has this reference. 'There's nothing more
perfect than nature,' she says. 'Observing nature inspires me, and
gives me the sensibility that I capture in my rugs'. They are crafted in
hand-tufted New Zealand wool.

1-3

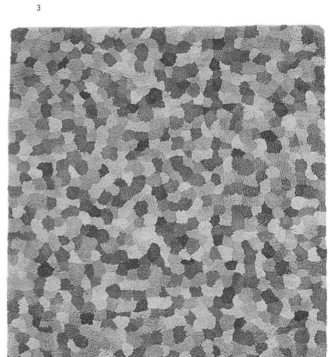

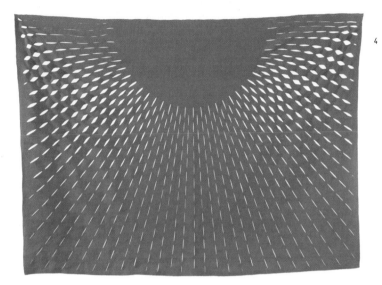

4

5

4-6 | The laser-cut Déployé series of
fabric throws was designed by Ana
Mir and Emili Padros, who work
collectively under the name Emiliana
Studio. The designers met in London
in 1992 when they were studying in
the industrial design programme at
Central St Martin's School of Art &
Design. In 1996 they founded their
studio in Barcelona where they work
together on a wide range of projects.

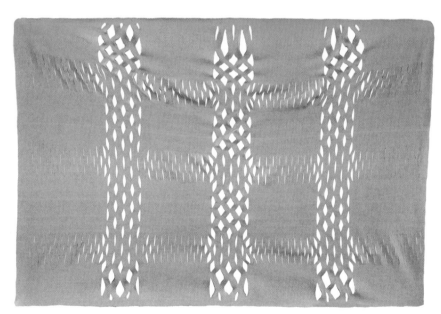

6

NINA JOBS

When someone in the Jobs family talks about textiles, people in Sweden always listen. But although her family tree boasts several generations of textile artists, Nina Jobs never had much to say about fabric when she was growing up. And with an education in graphic design and a masters degree in product design from the Ecole National Supérieure des Arts Décoratifs in Paris, Swedish textiles were the furthest thing from her mind when she set up her studio in Stockholm.

'My work is not specifically about fabrics,' Jobs says, 'it's about two-dimensional design, three-dimensional structures and product design. I'm more aware of what's going on in fashion and in furniture design than I am in the textile industry. I get ideas from travelling to overseas countries and hanging out in big cities.'

Much of Jobs' work is characterized by the impression of depth and movement it creates on a flat surface. 'I often work in different layers to create a 3-D feeling,' Jobs explains, 'and I often work with strong colours, sometimes overlapping them a little to create more depth. A pattern shouldn't feel static, because if it does it will seem banal. But it doesn't have to be complicated either. I like to keep my designs clean and simple. To create the "handmade" feeling, the patterns are never perfect, they always incorporate small mistakes!'

Jobs' textile work spread beyond Sweden's borders when she created the esteemed Jungle motif produced by David Design. Commissions from IKEA took her motifs to homes throughout the world, when patterns such as Hedvig and Kilan were printed on bed linens, and motifs such as Jutta and Petra were printed on interior textiles. 'The collaborations with IKEA gave me an opportunity to spread my designs worldwide, which I did with care and awareness,' Jobs says.

Some of the products Jobs has designed have required textiles engineered especially for them. The award-winning Urbana rain poncho, for example, which Jobs designed for Simplicitas, was created in collaboration with technologists based at the manufacturer. 'It took a lot of research to find the right thread for weaving the textiles, but it was worth it.' When Jobs designed the free-standing DoReMi screen for Abstract, she worked with a polyester blend made especially to create the rounded reliefs on the surface.

1 Nina Jobs believes that form, function and material should be combined, and her approach to textile design often results in schemes that map her motifs in three-dimensional space. Her Cosmos fabric is both interior upholstery and two-dimensional surface design.

2 A string of pearls inspired the designer's aptly named black-and-white Pearl motif.

3 Jobs combines heart motifs in shapes that resemble four-leaf clovers, in her Heart fabric.

Jobs' work is as popular with architects and interior designers as it is with retail consumers, and sometimes they use her motifs in unexpected ways. Her collaboration with Kitayama & Company and Cibone in Japan resulted in bold, graphic patterns that coloured the walls and ceilings of the interior. The prints seemed to create a tunnel for people to walk through, which gave an interactive dimension to the design. Projects like this contribute to a growing movement to create interactive products, which is taking textile design in an exciting new direction.

2

3

1

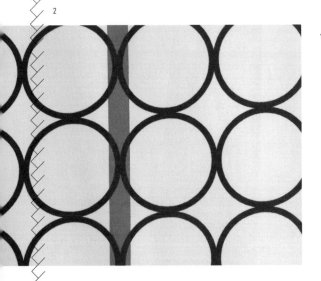

3

2

1&3   Jobs's Daisy fabric was commissioned
by IKEA and produced as the Hedda
Blom bed linen sets. The designer
created several versions of the pattern,
shown here in two colourways.

2   Geometric circle repeats and round
forms loom large in Jobs' work. Here,
the crisp outlines of black circles
are foiled by an azure blue stripe in
the background.

4   Like Jobs's Pearl motif, this black-and-white design evokes a beaded necklace.

5   Jobs says that her work is not specifically about fabrics, but about exploring two-dimensional design and creating three-dimensional structures. Her Jutta motif was inspired by architectural shapes and designed for interior fabrics.

6   She designed this floor cushion, covering it in one of her signature black-and-white motifs and embellishing it with red trim.

7   The Point motif features expansive circles that swell beyond their outlines.

1

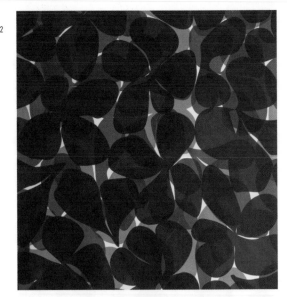

2

3

4

Jobs's Jungle fabrics were created by Swedish furniture manufacturer   1-2
David Design, where they were used for upholstery and lighting.

The shapes of letters were the inspiration for the typographical   3-4
Lowercase fabric design. They fit together like peas in a pod creating
a uniquely multi-directional repeat.

The Wind motif is based on high-velocity whirlwinds,   5
which Job's softened into swirling currents.

Jungle is a 'family' of fabrics created by overlaying individual motifs   6-7
to create new designs. When the black-and-white motif (6) is
combined with the green-and-ochre fabric (7) a darker, busier motif
is produced (2).

5

6

7

PETRA BLAISSE

At a time when nature is becoming central to urban expansion, the textile is becoming an integral part of contemporary architecture. Thanks to Petra Blaisse, the visionary Amsterdam-based designer behind the textile studio aptly named Inside Outside, exchanges between architectonic ideas, urban landscapes and fabric design are forging fresh directions. She works collaboratively with architects, preservationists and urban planners, creating textiles that take shape in response to volume, function and spatial proportions, and landscapes that transform bleak suburban sites into multi-layered gardens and tactile parks. Her architectural commissions, which include flooring design and technological initiatives, are almost always site-specific and, most of the time, Blaisse's work begins even before the architects have themselves broken ground.

Blaisse's input is making the modern cityscape a more beautiful place. The materials that she adds to architecture imbue the built environment with softness, a sense of movement, colour and tactility. Inside Outside's implementations have been described as 'warm', 'elegant', 'sensual' and 'female' – a direct contrast to descriptions such as 'static', 'male' or even 'cold' that often characterize contemporary architecture. That said, Blaisse's works are not intended to make architecture more feminine, but to introduce soft forms that harmonize with the architects' ambition to make buildings more fluid, labile and interactive.

Since establishing Inside Outside in 1991, Blaisse and her colleagues have created textiles for monumental buildings in virtually every corner of the globe. Rich in local influences that often bridge the cultural gap between local traditions and modern progress, her projects seem to weave whole worlds. 'Since our projects stretch from northern Europe to the Middle East, from China to Africa, and from the United States to South America, we've learned to adapt our perspective and mentality to suit local sites,' she explains. 'Even as close as southern Europe, we discover that the cultural language differs dramatically from our northern European point of view. Colour and symbols have different meanings among different peoples, and materials such as cloth, plants and soil vary from culture to culture, climate to climate and area to area. In some areas, use of a specific colour, flower or tree may be prohibited, and in another, the use of the

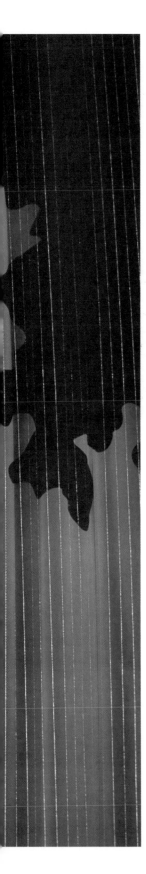

human figure or natural forms may be forbidden. Even something as universal as water can be considered to be a threatening force in one place, while it is a sublime symbol for wealth and wellbeing in another.'

While universal in scope, the appeal of Blaisse's work is not created merely through building cultural bridges. She thinks of cloth as a common denominator throughout the world. 'Textiles have connected all forms of human experience throughout mankind's shared history, and therefore they have cultural and emotional significance for almost everyone today,' she says. 'Time, fashions and environments create experiences, while textiles represent a global language of memory and emotions. These sensations are amplified by our textiles; because they are often large scale, they augment their effects. The textiles make almost everyone want to touch, smell and feel the fabrics, irrespective of their nationality, ethnic background or age.'

Blaisse and her colleagues begin commissions by gaining the broadest possible overview of the project. 'Like invisible rings, geopolitical influences ripple through the projects,' Blaisse explains. 'Issues such as climate change and water shortages need to be considered, together with the political and economic situation of a client, institution or country. We initiate exchanges with local inhabitants, specialists and institutions about the issues linked to our design brief. This form of research proves incredibly inspiring, and it influences the projects in ways that go far beyond it.' These local influences are then subtly expressed in the finished product, for example in the choices of colour, the type of yarn, the outline of an image or in the rhythm of a pattern.

While the textiles designed by Inside Outside fulfil a variety of functional and aesthetic roles, their sensory impact is central to the work, irrespective of whether the project is interior or exterior, small-scale or large. 'Apart from factors such as acoustics, lighting and climatic control, our curtains, carpets and wall- and ceiling-finishes play a part in the experience of a room, consciously and subconsciously, physically and psychologically,' Blaisse says. 'Their colour compositions and degree of reflection influence the light or shaded areas in a room. Their movements create air flow and soft sounds that change the visitors' experience of the size and shape of the space. Their scale, or the scale of their decorations, can change the scale of the building, its structure or the interior spaces. They can also communicate the function of a space and the cultural perception of a place – becoming its "face" to the world around it.'

Blaisse first gained ground in landscape design in 1992 when Inside Outside collaborated with French landscape designer Yves Brunier, who invited them to develop the Museumpark project in Rotterdam. Since then, Blaisse has designed landscapes in Seoul, Los Angeles and Milan. Her landscape designs are characterized by contrasting textures and winding abstractions. Seemingly conceived as large-scale motifs, Blaisse's gardens have more in common with land art than they do with urban design. 'The gardens and landscapes we design are not only about mapping, designing and organizing public space, but also about complexity, unpredictability, storytelling, secrecy and beauty,' she explains. 'They trigger the senses and stir the visitors' curiosity, while at the same time, they re-awaken memories and evoke sensations like surprise, awe, fear and delight.' Blaisse also finds that one of the most exciting aspects of landscape design is working with living forms that have the potential to outlive the designers: 'A plant or a garden usually needs years or decades to grow and mature, while a textile, on the other hand, starts to deteriorate as soon as you begin to use it.'

1 Petra Blaisse has mastered the art of creating holes in textiles, something designers traditionally avoided at all costs. By stitching rows of holes into the fabric, a subtle striped effect is created.

Landscape design comes naturally to Blaisse, who regards fabric surfaces as individual topographies. 'In textiles, a pleat creates a topography, and so does the knot, the tear, the hole, the textures of a weave and the microscopic fibres of a yarn,' she explains. 'All topographies, whether found in the natural landscape or in the surface of a textile, catch light, deflect wind, diffuse sound, or absorb all of these elements. They create shelter and also open up to form space. They forms boundaries and can choreograph movement, while at the same time inviting views, creating experiences of scale, vastness and perspective. Topography offers variety, establishes narratives and makes room for meditation, yet can manifest forms of power, and even the experience of vulnerability.'

As Blaisse continues to push design aesthetics forward, she also imbues her work with esoteric principles. She and her team are among the few design professionals who fully grasp what textiles represent historically, and what they can harbour, convey and exemplify today. 'I have discovered that our work is nothing less then a perpetual search for paradise,' she says. 'We work towards beauty, wellbeing and empathy. We visualize the life cycle and do our best to recreate it, literally and symbolically. The growth of a garden, the opening and closing of a drape and the passage of sunlight over a textile during a day represent the movement, change and deterioration that underpins the transition of all life.'

1&3 This green, finned, multi-functional 'darkening' curtain creates a soft wall that filters out sunlight, forming a light-dimming barrier while allowing visitors to peep through. It was designed for the Mercedes-Benz Museum, Stuttgart, in Germany.

2

2   A total of 17 workers in Germany and France came together to tear white voile into bands 10cm (4in) wide, zigzag the pieces through string netting and knot them together. Altogether, it took a total of 700 hours. The curtain was commissioned by the Casa da Música, in Porto, Portugal.

4   Blaisse's work is often characterized by contrasts, no matter how subtle. Here, dark and light fabrics sit side by side, as does a shiny texture and a matt one.

1   Long fibres like these 'brush hairs'
     scatter and disperse sound waves
     to create an acoustic atmosphere.
     The fibres were inserted into panels
     covered with gold-coloured metal foil.

2   Blaisse designed this fabric
     for a London penthouse to
     bring nature indoors through
     'a translucent curtain'.

3   These 'suncreening' and 'darkening'
     curtains were commissioned by
     the Casa da Música. They have
     tiny portals that enable them to
     filter light.

4-5   The hand-knotted filtering curtain
     shown previously (page 271) is not
     a woven textile. The loosely-knotted
     strips of fabrics that they are made of
     'float' within the warp, breaking away
     from the idea that a textile must be
     tightly woven.

4

5

1

2

1 The filtering curtain was partially inspired by the white mist that rolls in from the coast around Porto. When the curtain is lowered, it moves in the same ethereal manner.

2 Blaisse was commissioned to make curtains that look good even in the dark.

3 In her work, architecture and textiles meet literally and metaphorically as illustrated by this blueprint motif.

4

3

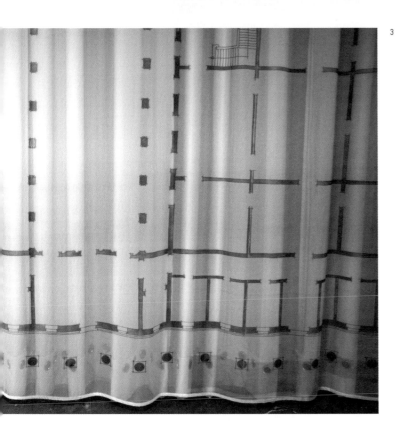

4 This curtain for the Mick Jagger Performing Arts Centre is constructed fromvertical bands of pink velvet overlaid with alternate vertical bands of gauze.

PUBLISHER TEXTILES

There's an image of an old-fashioned typewriter in Publisher Textiles' logo, and it hints at a story waiting to be written. When Mark and Rhynie Cawood established the company in Sydney in 2002, they formed a creative team that could take part in every aspect of the textile process. Since then, they have designed a variety of sumptuous one-offs, limited edition interior fabrics and printed upholstery repeats. Each design is screen printed in the studio by hand, using classical techniques such as devoré, overprinting and masking. The duo regularly experiment with processes using metallics, dyes and resists, and the fabrics that result are completely unique.

At a time when industrially-printed fabrics are the norm, establishing a textile studio powered only by hand-production may have seemed anachronistic to some. 'Industrial printing was never an option for us,' explains Rhynie Cawood, 'because our designs take time to grow. We don't have an exact image of what the finished designs will look like, they just develop organically throughout the process while we are printing and producing them. We really enjoy being involved in every step of the process, and being so hands-on gives us the control to change bits as we go along.'

Some of Publisher's techniques are so specialized that it's almost impossible to achieve the same effect a season later, while others have been perfected to the extent that the same effects can be created on a variety of materials. 'We once covered a wing chair in an acid-etched denim we called "Arachnid", which was created using a technique we originally developed for fashion textiles,' Cawood explains. 'Up close, you can see how the brown section of the print actually begins where the top layer of indigo was eaten away. The print is a damask version of a spider, which, together with the worn denim, creates an old look that feels new when you touch it.' Also printed on damask, their Psycat design is another eye-catching textile. 'The print is a collection of inkblot butterfly shapes which reminded us of the Rorschach inkblot test used by psychologists. The scratchy texture around the motifs combines an Ikat dye technique with a damask style.' The retro-like Crackers fabric resulted from a technical challenge that led to a new development in their colour-printing technique. 'We wanted to create a five-colour print by using as few screens as possible,' Cawood explains. 'In the end, we managed to do it with only three screens.'

Shortly after Publisher Textiles started producing hand-printed repeats, they decided to establish a line of printed artworks. 'We were printing skirts on a lay-cloth, and there were areas where the prints had overlapped onto it,' Cawood explains. 'Over time, all the dyes layered together and created an interesting effect. That inspired us to experiment with layering images and printing them by using different pressures. We got some primed artist's canvases and tried it out on them, and the technique eventually developed into the range of printed artworks we sell today.'

When the story of Publisher Textiles is finally written, it will certainly have a happy ending. 'Our way of working has been a personal choice,' Cawood says, 'and Mark and I have finally found our home. You carve your own path and the world will respond...need I say more?'

1 From their base in Sydney, Publisher Textiles design the sumptuous one-offs, limited edition fabrics and printed repeats that are admired around the world. Their fabrics are screen-printed in the studio by hand, using classical techniques. They often create new processes using metallic pigments, dyes and resists. The Bugsey motif, printed on a cotton/linen blend in a variety of colourways, is one of their signature fabrics.

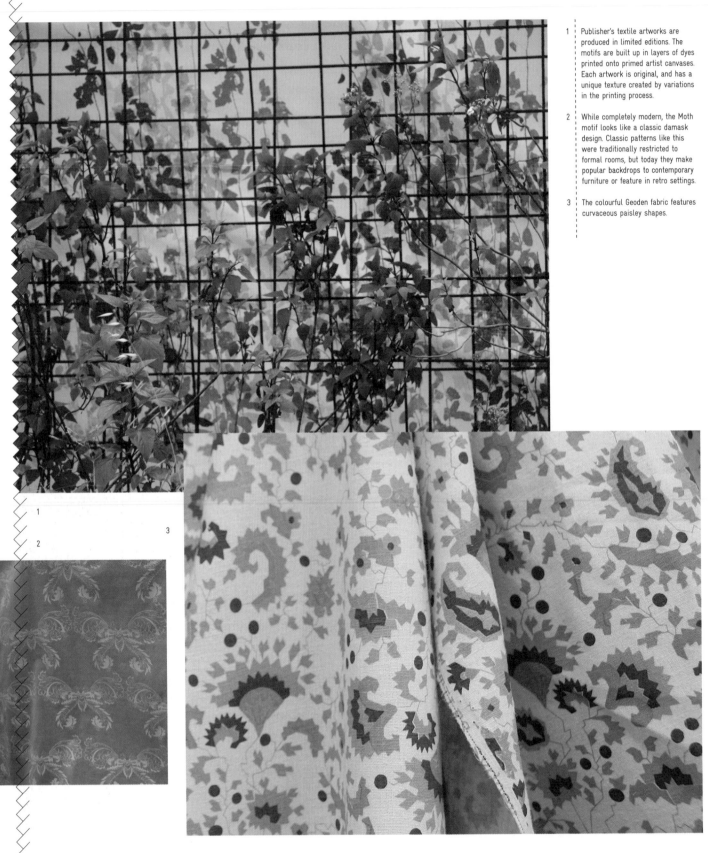

1   Publisher's textile artworks are produced in limited editions. The motifs are built up in layers of dyes printed onto primed artist canvases. Each artwork is original, and has a unique texture created by variations in the printing process.

2   While completely modern, the Moth motif looks like a classic damask design. Classic patterns like this were traditionally restricted to formal rooms, but today they make popular backdrops to contemporary furniture or feature in retro settings.

3   The colourful Geoden fabric features curvaceous paisley shapes.

1

2

3

4 Apollo is one of the most powerful gods in Greek mythology. The Apollo textile (left) is equally compelling in its commanding radial motifs. The Psycat design (right) is based on inkblot butterfly shapes reminiscent of the Rorschach inkblot test used by psychologists.

1

2

The Botanica textile brings 1
botanical illustrations to mind,
capturing the crisp outlines of
flora and fauna in a variety of
colourways and fabrics.

Publisher covered this wing chair 2
in their Arachnid design, an acid–
etched denim originally created for
fashion textiles. The design is a
damask print that appears to
be antique when printed on
worn denim.

3   The Bugsey motif shown previously
(page 277), printed here in black.

4   Publisher's stylish motifs are also in
vogue in the fashion world, and are
printed onto garments and accessories.

3

4

1

2

3

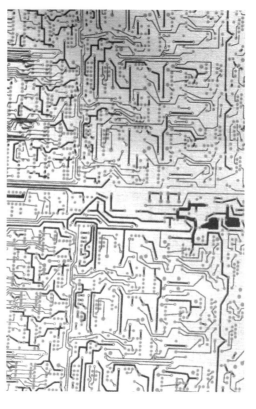

1   Some of Publisher's techniques are so specialized that it's almost impossible to achieve the same effect a season later, while others have been perfected to the extent that the same effects can be created on a variety of materials.

2   All Publisher's cushions are made with natural fabrics. Printed fabric is used for the cushions' front panel, paired with a contrasting monochrome back panel.

3   Publisher's eschew industrial processes, using traditional techniques and handcraft methods instead. Their Circuit design references hi-tech production in its motif, but the studio plans to remain faithful to its lo-tech, eco-friendly ethos.

SARI
SYVÄLUOMA

Since Finnish designer Sari Syväluoma moved to Norway in 1994, the Norwegian textile scene has changed forever. Despite its long history of colourful embroideries and elaborate folk costumes, Norway had never had a tradition of printed textiles that reflected contemporary sensibilities. When she accepted the role of textile designer at Sellgrens Veveri AS, Syväluoma introduced a range of expressive, eye-catching designs that had never before been produced in Norway. Since then, her work has put Norwegian textiles on the map. Her woven jacquards and printed fabrics have been exported internationally and even exhibited by the Norwegian Ministry of Foreign Affairs as examples of outstanding textile design.

'Not bad for a young Finnish designer, eh?' chides Syväluoma from her studio in Oslo, as she reflects on what she's achieved. 'I was so happy to come to Norway and contribute with something that was really needed here then. When I came here, the government was just starting to promote good design and make it possible for young designers to show their work abroad. It's exciting to be part of a new movement and see how the design scene here is starting to catch up with its Nordic neighbours.'

Syväluoma says she designs 'just for fun', because she regards textile design as a playful medium. Her work is characterized by a palate of soft colours, which she builds up in layers with the careful composition of a still life. She consciously creates whimsical motifs or casually sketches patterns so vibrant that the repeat seems to disappear altogether. 'I would describe my style as quirky,' she says. 'I love organic shapes and free-flowing patterns. I like contrast in colours, shapes and material.'

Contemporary Nordic interiors are often minimal, and Syväluoma likes to counteract cool decor with powerful patterns that hold their own in the interior, eclipsing the need for paint finishes, elaborate carpets and decorative detailing. 'My fabrics are designed to be draped across chairs, sofas, beds and windows,' Syväluoma says. 'They are intended to be a functional art form for the home, something that can say something about the personality of the person living there. I tell people: "think of your home as your universe, filled with the things you love, things that tell the story of you".'

Today, Syväluoma works primarily as a freelance designer who also embarks on partnerships with other practitioners. She produces small-edition print runs for interior design boutiques and launched a range of children's textiles in 2006. In recent years, she has expanded her client base to create interior fabrics for manufacturers in Britain, Germany, Finland and Hong Kong, but Syväluoma says she is not done with Norway yet. 'A lot of my work is exported as "Norwegian Design", and that's fine,' she says. 'But my real work now is to bring more international influences into Norway, so that the people here can experience something more than just Nordic design.'

1 Sari Syväluoma thinks of textile design as a playful medium,
   and a source of fun. Her work often features vibrant colours,
   which she builds up in layers as if composing a fabric still life.

2 Her Branches motif has been printed on a variety of textiles
   and interior accessories, shown here on cotton bed linen.

3 She designed a collection of motifs for babies and young children.
   The prints feature colourful, cartoon-like motifs for furniture, bedding,
   wall-hangings and clothing.

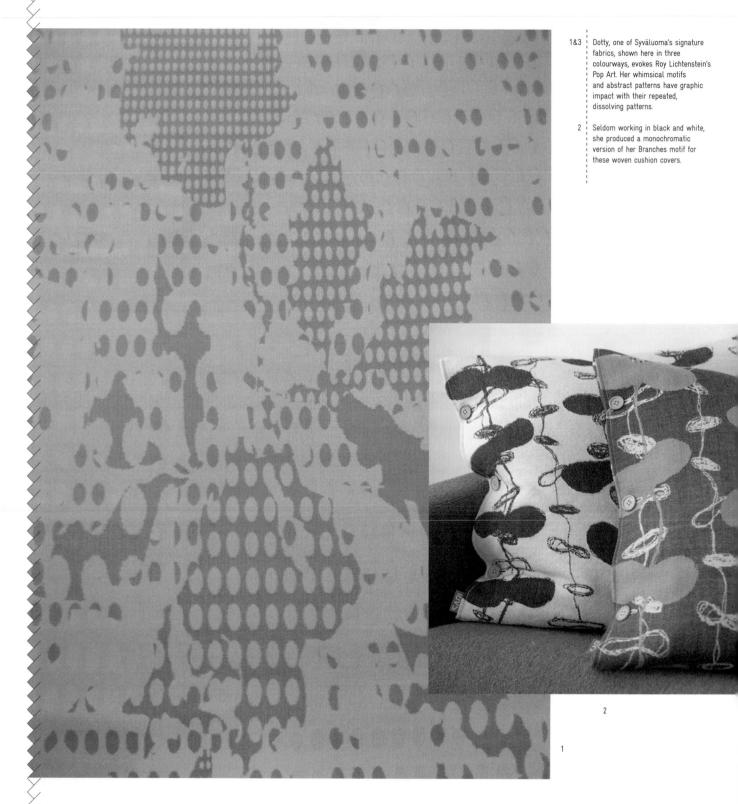

1&3 Dotty, one of Syväluoma's signature fabrics, shown here in three colourways, evokes Roy Lichtenstein's Pop Art. Her whimsical motifs and abstract patterns have graphic impact with their repeated, dissolving patterns.

2 Seldom working in black and white, she produced a monochromatic version of her Branches motif for these woven cushion covers.

2

1

3

4

4 | The designer's Flowers in the Landscape fabric repeat is shown here as a wall hanging and cushion covers. She sets out to produce powerful patterns that can hold their own in the interior, eliminating the need for wallpaper and other surface treatments.

1   Syväluoma's Dotty fabric, in yellow
    and coral pink woven in lurex and
    wool, complements her Rose motif.

2   An autumnal version of the Dotty
    design embellished with falling oak
    leaves and acorns.

3-4 The designer produced upholstery
    fabric for children's furniture
    designed by Johan Orbeck Aase.
    The two designers teamed up to
    contribute to the 'Designers go
    Playground', project, creating a
    design concept that would appeal
    to children and adults alike.

1

2

3

4

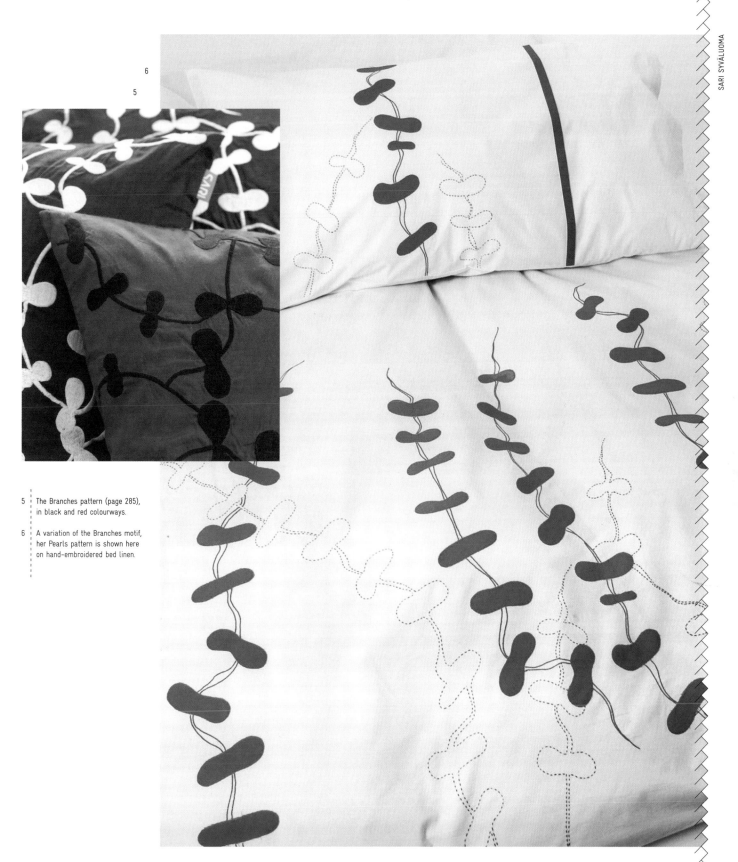

5　The Branches pattern (page 285), in black and red colourways.

6　A variation of the Branches motif, her Pearls pattern is shown here on hand-embroidered bed linen.

The See Me motif has rich textures and raised dots that evoke words written in Braille. The fabric is shown here in cushion covers and curtain fabric.   1

This close up of See Me reveals how densely textured the fabric is.   2

A version of Dotty, seen here in contrasting colourways.   3

4   One of Syväluoma's children's motifs is shown here with a green background. The motifs are intended to be 'functional and fun'.

5   A portrait of the designer, photographed in her own home with her Branches fabric in the background. Syväluoma encourages others to 'think of your home as your universe, filled with the things you love, things that tell the story of you'.

6   A version of Dotty printed with a monochrome background.

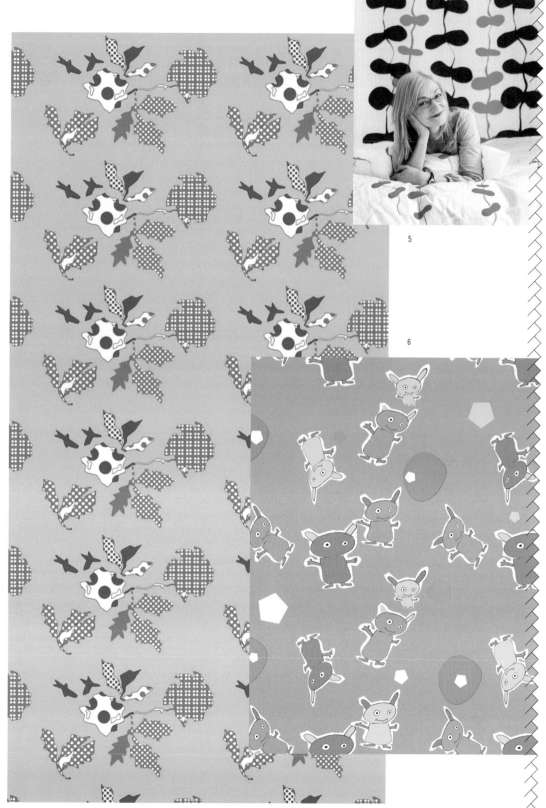

4

5

6

SOPHIE MALLEBRANCHE ----------

The textiles produced by Paris-based designer Sophie Mallebranche are often compared to the forces of nature – words such as 'whirlwind' and 'volcanic' have been used to describe her work in the past – but anyone who has ever met Mallebranche knows that her work is actually about the calm rather than the storm.

Mallebranche's fabrics are atmospheric and evocative without striving for effect. Her works are born out of understated sentiments, but they make strong statements. 'You could say that while I work, my mind is absorbed by a world of five square inches,' Mallebranche says, 'but my intention is to lead the person who will touch my fabric to a dimension far beyond that. I need to go beyond the material properties of the textile I'm creating, to a place created by mystery and imagination.'

In Mallebranche's world, textiles are not limited to surface expressions. Refusing to recognize differentiation between body, space and textiles, she takes human perception as her starting point and uses her work as a catalyst for expanding it. 'My challenge is to create three-dimensionally with a material that is often regarded as two-dimensional,' she says. 'I believe in extending the boundaries of textiles far beyond functionality. To do that, I search for sensitive materials, because it's essential to find the right way to integrate light, colour and texture. Then I try to introduce dream, poetry and mystery.'

While Mallebranche's textiles may be born out of dreamy reverie, they are anchored to chic environments once they emerge into the physical world. Her works have been commissioned by luxury retailers such as Guerlain, leading hoteliers such the Hôtel Plaza Athénée Paris, legendary restaurants such as Drugstore Publicis on the Champs-Elysées and some impressive penthouse apartments in Manhattan's Upper East Side. 'Most of the time I bring something theatrical to the space,' Mallebranche says. 'At that scale, my creations can be considered to be architectural elements or interior textures. My starting point is to make an interesting response to the space. Then I concentrate on the joy of experimentation until I find solutions that may surprise myself.'

Mallebranche's experimentation with metal fibres has earned her a reputation as a material innovator. With the acumen of a metalsmith, she tools metal fibres into

1-2 Sophie Mallebranche creates lustrous woven fabrics by weaving copper, stainless steel, bronze or brass with plant fibres and synthetic materials. Her adeptness at tooling metal fibres into gossamer mesh has earned her a reputation as a material innovator and a top designer, although she defines herself foremost as an artist.

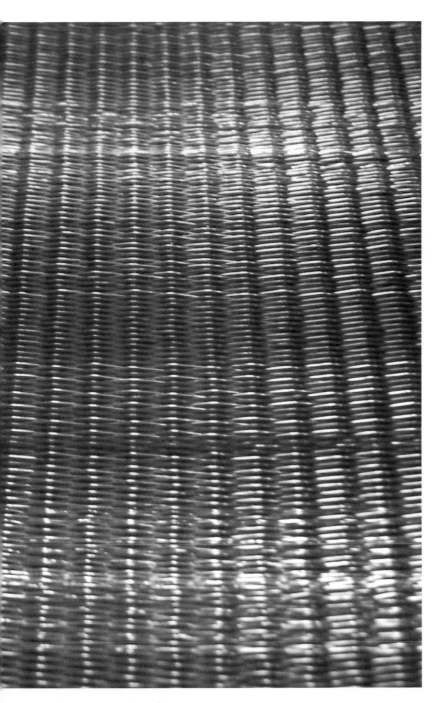

gossamer meshes that come alive in the passing light. 'I grew up with a fascination for metals,' she says. 'As a child I played in the kitchen of my family's restaurant in Normandy, dashing between enamelled refrigerators, stainless steel workbenches and copper pans. Much later, when I was a student at the Duperré School of Applied Arts in Paris, I was still influenced by the kitchen environment. My thesis examined how one could bring sensitive awareness to the materials used in refrigerators merely by transforming them into something else. I thought it could be achieved by trying to weave these unusual materials, which were created in the second industrial revolution. So finding a sensitive expression for metals became my own artistic vocabulary.'

Although Mallebranche interprets modern metals through ancient craft traditions, she is aware that they present both environmental hazards and sustainable solutions. 'For sure I'm concerned about the quality, durability and environmental impact of metals,' she says, 'but they have other properties too. Because they can conduct energy, electromagnetic impulses and acoustic phonetics, they have the potential to give textiles these characteristics. Their capacity for transmitting solar energy is promising – I can imagine designing a curtain which is able to transform solar energy into light or heat. I may not be able to take these things forward when I work with fabrics today, but that's okay. I'm still focused on creating the textiles of tomorrow.'

1 | Mallebranche's stunningly beautiful bejeweled fabrics have more in common with jewellery design than they do with traditional textiles. She embellishes the surfaces of her metal fabrics with glass and crystal, creating cascading patterns that radiate in the ambient light.

2 | Textiles like this one reveal the lustrous colours and shimmering surfaces that copper wire can create, ranging from burnished reds to golden yellows.

3 | By weaving thin strands of silver and stainless steel into panels of fabric, Mallebranche creates designs that combine delicate textile art with robust architectural materials. Standard panels are usually around one metre wide, but most of her fabrics are custom-made.

4 | Her starting point is to make a response to the space for which she will produce work. Most of her textiles are made in large scale, and are architectural by nature.

3

4

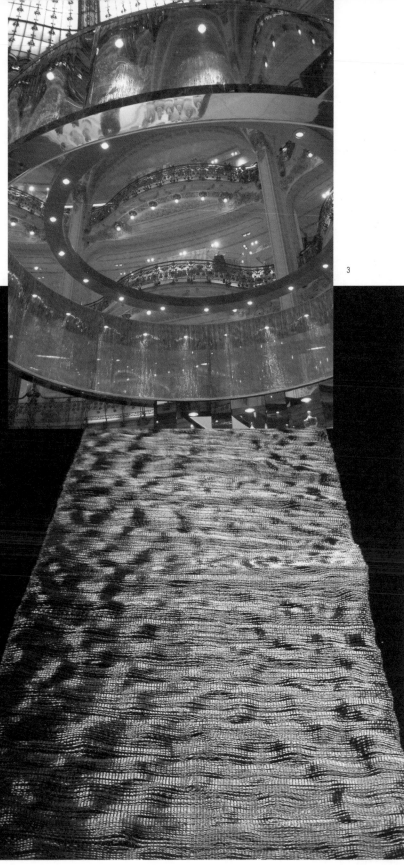

1

2

3

Mallebranche was commissioned by
French fragrance house Guerlain to
create textile installations for their
boutique at Galeries Lafayette in
Paris. Her textiles lit up the boutique,
radiating copper-coloured rays
throughout the space.

1–2

She created this loosely woven
metal fibre textile for a 'soft
wall' installation in a residential
apartment in Manhattan, New York.

3

6

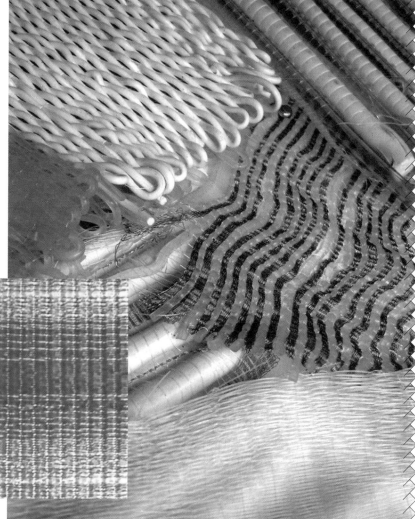

4   She was commissioned to create
    contemporary window treatments
    for the restaurant at the Hôtel Plaza
    Athénée in Paris. The textiles were
    woven variously in stainless steel
    and copper.

5   A variety of natural fibres and
    synthetic materials are interwoven
    with Mallebranche's metal materials.
    Linen, nylon, silk and moulded
    silicone are also added to increase
    the fabric's ductility.

6   Detail of her copper fabric
    (pages 292–3).

TIMOROUS BEASTIES

Sometimes Timorous Beasties disappoint their customers. Despite the sell-out success of their striking textiles, it's not unusual for customers to storm out of the showroom in a huff, or ring to say that they're returning their purchases. Like magnets, their traditional toile de Jouy fabrics and naturalistic repeats attract orders from around Britain and abroad. But sometimes customers, expecting them to depict classic eighteenth-century imagery, feel repelled by what they see close up.

Toile designs such as Glasgow Toile and London Toile present derisive visions of these cities. 'Glasgow' is seen teeming with drug addicts, prostitutes and drunks, depicted against a backdrop of crumbling tower blocks and marauding seagulls, while 'London' features repeats that depict a man holding a young woman at gunpoint. While these scenes are regarded as unconventional today, their frosty reception is nothing new. Original French toiles from the eighteenth century were equally shocking in their scenes of womanizing, smoking and drinking.

When Paul Simmons and Alistair McAuley established Timorous Beasties, their Glasgow-based textile studio in 1990, they did not set out to be conventional in any way. They named the new company after an expression found in Robert Burns' poem 'To a Mouse', which goes like this: 'Wee, sleekit, cowrin', tim'rous beastie, O, what a panic's in thy breastie'.

According to McAuley, the name suited them, 'not because we're at all timid, but because we wanted to call our company something that had nothing to do with us and didn't reflect what we did in any way. From the outset, our studio was a collaborative effort and we always planned to produce things other than fabric. So there was no point in being called "Simmons and McAuley Fabrics Ltd" when we work collaboratively and also produce wallpaper and interior products. And Timorous Beasties has a nicer ring to it than our names do.'

With their mugger motifs, fly fabrics and womanizing wallpaper, these two Scotsmen have rocked the boat of 'good taste' floating in the interior design industry's tepid waters. 'Even when we were students we hated floral fabrics,' McAuley says. 'We graduated at a time when floral prints were mostly horrendous redrawings of archival work or badly drawn action repeats of soft, fluffy pastel

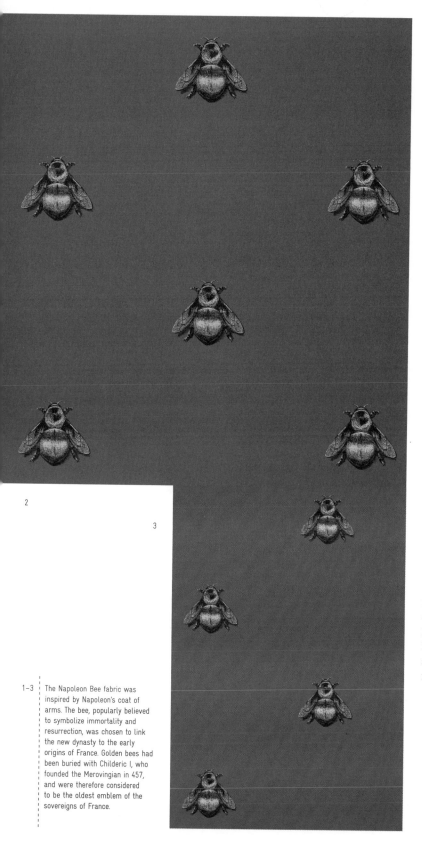

2

3

1–3 The Napoleon Bee fabric was inspired by Napoleon's coat of arms. The bee, popularly believed to symbolize immortality and resurrection, was chosen to link the new dynasty to the early origins of France. Golden bees had been buried with Childeric I, who founded the Merovingian in 457, and were therefore considered to be the oldest emblem of the sovereigns of France.

flowers. The natural world is such a fantastic resource for a textile designer. We couldn't believe how designers just fucked it up by producing bastardized versions of flower motifs.'

Because both McAuley and Simmons possessed a passion for drawing, it felt natural to them to sketch out motifs by hand rather than take a graphic approach. 'Part of the appeal of seventeenth- and eighteenth-century toiles is all the work that went into drawing them,' McAuley says. 'I've noticed people comment on how labour intensive and controlled our toiles are. William Morris's legacy is a similar thing, all the details are painstakingly true to reality.'

McAuley and Simmons look for detailed depictions of nature to guide their choices of motifs. 'I guess nature is a classic inspiration for textile designers,' McAuley says. 'We look at botany, entomology and zoology for things that look edgy but don't date. It's about bringing the outside world inside. When it comes to using thistles, the national symbol of Scotland, I guess we're doffing our caps to Scottishness. After all, we have a great history of design up here.'

McAuley says that Timorous Beasties' rapid expansion has made work much more enjoyable, because they've been able to open retail boutiques and outsource the production to local manufacturers. 'Our growth has taken us out of our comfort zone, and that's the best thing that could have happened to us. We can channel our profits into developing new types of work, and since we outsource most of our production now, we can use the studio just for complicated hand printing that we can't get done anywhere else.'

Timorous Beasties' next ventures will be a range of lace and a line of jacquards, and they have undertaken architectural commissions that involve etching their motifs deep into 40-metre- (130-foot-) long slabs of quarried slate. 'I'm fascinated by how companies like Emporio Armani can move into interior design and have great success just because they've established a strong brand in another area. It makes me think "Why not launch a Timorous Beasties perfume?".'

1–3 Butterfly wings feature some of the most beautiful motifs found in the natural world, making them perfect subjects for textile motifs. Timorous Beasties' Butterfly pattern, shown here in a variety of wallpaper colourways, highlights their velvety beauty.

1

2

3

4   The bee and butterfly themes of Timorous Beasties' pattern repeats was extended into their Insect wallpaper, which features moths, beetles and other creepy crawlies.

5   The Japanese Tree fabric recalls the cherry trees that bow gracefully over the Japanese landscape. Renowned for their elegant outlines, they are an ideal choice for textile design.

4

5

1

1-2 Timorous Beasties' flock wallpaper
collection brings velvety textures
to wall surfaces. Their Devil
Damask design subtly morphs a
traditional outline into a Chinese
dragon motif.

3-6 Timorous Beasties' damask fabrics
update a time-honoured textile
form for the contemporary interior.
Damask fabrics are popular
for the subtle surface textures
that reflect the light differently
according to the angle of the rays
that pass over it.

2

3

4

5

6

1 Timorous Beasties' Glasgow toile
fabric reinterprets traditional
toile with an urban twist for the
twenty-first century. The motifs
depict drug users, prostitutes and
drunks, shown against a backdrop
of crumbling tower blocks and
marauding seagulls.

2-3 The toile fabrics are made into
a variety of interior accessories,
such as lampshades.

1

3

2

4

5

4-5 | The London toile fabric, like the
Glasgow toile (page 304), is a
contemporary interpretation of a
classic form. It features repeats
that depict a man holding a young
woman at gunpoint.

1. Thistles are the national symbol of Scotland, and Timorous Beasties relish in their Scottish roots. 'After all, we have a great history of design up here,' they said. This Thistle motif is from their lace collection, shown here in ivory.

2. The Hot House motif, also in the lace collection, in black.

3. The Devil Damask design, shown previously in a wallpaper version (page 302), is also produced in fabric for their lace collection.

4. The Oriental Orchid motifs merge the exotic with the everyday.

5. The Grecian vase is right at home among Timorous Beasties' visual cannon of awesome gods, daring heroes and fabulous monsters. Their Vertical Vase fabric design, shown here in Ivory Madras, is part of their lace collection.

4

5

1–2 | William Morris' legacy can be identified in a few of Timorous Beasties' floral prints, as this McGegan Rose motif, shown here on wallpaper, reveals.

3–5 | Pheasants have long been a symbol of British country life, but their role as a visual icon originates in ancient China, where they were embroidered into the robes of court officials. Timorous Beasties' Pheasant motifs evoke eighteenth-century Chinoiserie designs, harkening back to their Eastern roots.

2

3

4

5

3

4

5

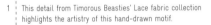

1   This detail from Timorous Beasties' Lace fabric collection
     highlights the artistry of this hand-drawn motif.

2   Because iguanas spend most of their lives in the treetops,
     descending to earth only infrequently to mate, lay eggs, or
     change trees, they seem perfectly at home amidst birds and
     airborne insects, as Timorous Beasties' Iguana motif illustrates.

3–4 The Tree of Life appears in myths and folklore traditions,
     and through the centuries have featured in many European
     interiors. Timorous Beasties' design of this name perpetuates
     that tradition today.

5   Timorous Beasties' Thistle pattern, seen previously (page 306),
     is shown here on wallpaper.

DIRECTORY

DESIGNER DIRECTORY

Anita Ahuja
A-78 Sector 63
NOIDA UP-201301
India
tel +91 120 421 6144
fax +91 120 421 6393
anita@conserveindia.org
www.conserveindia.org

Sébastien Barilleau
Cécile Henri Atelier
15 imp Primevères
75011 Paris
France
tel +33 1 43 57 04 07
fax +33 1 48 06 91 87
cecile.henri@wanadoo.fr

Thea Bjerg
Herman Triers Plads 5, 2tv
DK-1631 V Copenhagen
Denmark
tel +45 2068 6465
tb@theabjerg.com
www.theabjerg.com

Petra Blaisse
Inside Outside
1e Nassaustraat 5
1052 BD Amsterdam
The Netherlands
tel +31 20 6810 801
fax +31 20 6810 466
office@insideoutside.nl
www.insideoutside.nl

Johan Carpner
Johan Carpner Design AB
Box 12153
102 25 Stockholm
Sweden
tel +46 08 640 2140
www.johancarpner.se
johan@carpner.se

Luisa Cevese
Riedizioni
Via San Maurilio 3
Milan 20123
Italy
tel +39 02 801088
info@riedizioni.com
www.riedizioni.com

Angel Chang
511 West 25th Street
Suite 302
New York
NY 10001
USA
tel +1 212 941 5503
fax +1 212 813 3240
info@angelchang.com
www.angelchang.com

Natalie Chanin
462 Lane Drive
Florence
Alabama 35630
USA
tel +1 256 760 1090
office@alabamachanin.com
www.alabamachanin.com

c.neeon
Sewanstrasse 122
10319 Berlin
Germany
tel: +49 30 42105479
fax: +49 30 42105478
info@cneeon.de
www.cneeon.de

Camilla Diedrich
Studio Diedrich
Klippgatan 19A
S-116 35 Stockholm
Sweden
mob +46 73 3307 159
info@diedrich.se
www.diedrich.se

Hil Driessen	Driessen + van Deijne
	Atelier 27
	Stavangerweg 890
	1013 AX Amsterdam
	The Netherlands
	tel +31 20 686 9631
	mob +31 651 661 997
	info@hildriessen.com
	www.hildriessen.com

Hil Driessen
Driessen + van Deijne
Atelier 27
Stavangerweg 890
1013 AX Amsterdam
The Netherlands
tel +31 20 686 9631
mob +31 651 661 997
info@hildriessen.com
www.hildriessen.com

Becky Earley
Chelsea College of Art and Design
16 John Islip Street
London SW1P 4RJ
United Kingdom
tel +44 20 8994 4209
mob +44 7952 752 966
r.l.earley@chelsea.arts.ac.uk
www.beckyearley.com

Carlene Edwards
mob +44 7960 370 589
carlene@carlene-edwards.co.uk
www.carlene-edwards.co.uk

Shelley Fox
shelleyfox@shelleyfox.com
www.shelleyfox.com

Márcia Ganem
Rua das Laranjeiras, 10 - Pelourinho
40.026-230
Salvador, Bahia
Brazil
tel +55 71 3322 0234
mob +55 71 8812 5270
comunicacao@marciaganem.com.br
www.marciaganem.com.br

Kate Goldsworthy
34A Goldsboro Road
London SW8 4RR
United Kingdom
tel +44 20 7819 9972
mob +44 7974 725 119
hello@kategoldsworthy.co.uk
www.kategoldsworthy.co.uk

DESIGNER DIRECTORY

Gut's Dynamite Cabarets

Gut's Dynamite Cabarets
tel +81 80 6763 0935
info@g-d-cabarets.jp
www.g-d-cabarets.jp

Helena Hietanen

Apollonkatu 13 E 8
00100 Helsinki 100
Finland
tel +35 8505 366 184
helena.hietanen@saunalahti.fi

Claudia Hill

511 Avenue of the Americas
Suite 613
New York
NY 10011−8436
USA
tel +1 212 504 2809
info@claudiahill.com
www.claudiahill.com

Nina Jobs

Kreation Nina Jobs
Surbrunnsgatan 28
S-113 48 Stockholm
Sweden
tel +46 8 650 0523
mob +46 70 7141 475
info@ninajobs.se
www.ninajobs.se

Astrid Krogh

Dag Hammarskjölds Allé 7, 5 Tv
2100 Copenhagen
Denmark
tel +45 20 82 37 71
info@astridkrogh.com
www.astridkrogh.com

Loop

8 Springfield House
5 Tyssen Street
London E8 2LY
United Kingdom
tel +44 20 7812 9188
loop@loop.ph
www.loop.ph

Maija Louekari

maija@maijalouekari.com
www.maijalouekari.com

Kahori Maki

k@k-maki.com
www.k-maki.com

Sophie Mallebranche

Eh Oui
72 Rue du Faubourg Saint Honoré
75008 Paris
France
tel +33 6 1148 5836
contact@sophiemallebranche.com
www.sophiemallebranche.com

Florence Manlik

manlik.florence@neuf.fr
www.manlik.blogspot.com

Nani Marquina

Església 10, 3er D
08024 Barcelona
Spain
tel +34 932 376 465
fax +34 932 175 774
info@nanimarquina.com
www.nanimarquina.com

Karen Nicol

www.karennicol.com

Anne Kyyrö Quinn

Unit 2.06
OXO Tower Wharf
Bargehouse Street
London SE1 9PH
United Kingdom
tel +44 20 7021 0702
fax +44 20 7021 0770
info@annekyyroquinn.com

Alex Russell

LCB Depot (A302)
31 Rutland Street
Leicester LE1 1RE
United Kingdom
alex@alexrussell.com
www.alexrussell.com

Sari Syväluoma
Maridalsveien 56
0458 Oslo
Norway
mob +47 9309 4515
info@syvaluoma.com
www.sari-syvaluoma.com

Publisher Textiles
Unit 1
87 Moore Street
Leichhardt
NSW 2040
Australia
tel +61 2 9569 6044
fax +61 2 9569 6144
info@publishertextiles.com.au
www.publishertextiles.com.au

Timorous Beasties
46 Amwell Street
London EC1R 1XS
United Kingdom
tel +44 20 7833 5010
fax +44 20 7833 8010
london@timorousbeasties.com
www.timorousbeasties.com

Clare Tough
Adam Iezzi PR
tel +44 20 7287 1314
adam@aipr.co.uk

Hsiao-Chi Tsai
mob +44 7900 810 576
hsiao_chi_tsai@hotmail.com
www.hsiaochikimiya.com

Hanna Werning
Spring Street Studio AB
Drottninggatan 88D 1tr
SE-111 36 Stockholm
Sweden
tel +46 70 236 57 25
hello@byhanna.com
www.byhanna.com

INDEX

CREDITS

PICTURE CREDITS

The publisher would like to thank the following for permission to reproduce images in this book: pp 5 (left), 7 (vertical), 9 (vertical left), 10 (horizontal), 12–19: courtesy Alex Russell; pp 20–7: courtesy Angel Chang/photo credits: Dan Lecca, Lee Clower; pp 28–31: courtesy Anita Ahuja, Conserve India; pp 32–9: courtesy Becky Earley/photo credits: Tom Gidley, Paul Harris, Crafts Council, Becky Earley; pp 9 (middle right), 11 (horizontal), 40–51, 313 (bottom left): courtesy c.neeon; pp 52–7: courtesy Carlene Edwards; pp 58–67: courtesy AIPR/photo credit: Chris Moore; pp 68–73: courtesy Claudia Hill/photo credits: Assaf Evron, Ariko; pp 9 (horizontal top), 74–81: courtesy Florence Manlink/photo credits: Robert Normand, Florence Manlik; pp 82–91: courtesy Gut's Dynamite Cabarets; pp 9 (bottom left), 10 (vertical), 92–9, 313 (horizontal top), 315: courtesy Hanna Werning; pp 9 (top right), 11 (vertical), 100–7: courtesy Kahori Maki/photo credits: Becky Yee, Gyslain Yarhi; pp 108–15: courtesy Karen Nicol/photo credits: Karen Nicol, Tim Griffiths; pp 116–9: courtesy Luisa Cevese Riedizioni/photo credit: Luisa Cevese Riedizioni; pp 120–7: courtesy Márcia Ganem/photo credit: Ricardo Fernandes; pp 128–37: courtesy Natalie Chanin/photo credits: Robert Rausch, Peter Stangelmayr; pp 138–41: courtesy Cécile Henri Atelier/photo credits: Copyright Cécile Henri Atelier, Copyright Studio Mil Pat; pp 142–53: courtesy Shelley Fox/photo credits: Gavin Fernand, Lon Van Keulen, Chris Moore, Keith Paisley, Ellie Laycock, Shelley Fox, Rebecca & Mike, Ravi Deepres, Wilson Kao, Henry Hilsky; pp 154–63: courtesy Thea Bjerg/photo credit: Jeppe Gudmundsen-Holmgreen; pp 168 –71: courtesy Anne Kyyrö Quinn; pp 172–83: courtesy Astrid Krogh/photo credit: Torben Eskerod, Kurt Rodahl, Anders Sune Berg, Ole Hein Pedersen; pp 165 (far left and vertical left), 184–91: courtesy Camilla Diedrich/photo credits: Bengt Wanselius, Christopher Kovac, Louise Billgert, Rotaliana, Kvadrat; pp 165 (horizontal top), 192–5: courtesy Helena Hietanen/photo credit: Markku Alatalo/Studio Markku Alatalo Oy; pp 196–205: courtesy Hil Driessen, Bas van Pelt and The Museum at the Fashion Institute of Technology, New York/photo credits: Michiel Vijselaar, Eline Klein, Jan-Willem Steenmeijer, Jennifer Park (Courtesy FIT), VPT versteeg (Heusden), Cornbreadworks, Frank Visser, Hil Driessen, Rene de Wit; pp 206–15: courtesy Hsiao-Chi Tsai/photo credits: Hsiao-Chi Tsai, Ryosuke Kawana (make-up by Lisa Prentis), Hee Seung Chung, Kimiya Yoshikawa; pp 165 (vertical right), 167 (vertical), 216–23, 313 (vertical and horizontal middle): courtesy Johan Carpner; pp 224–31: courtesy Kate Goldsworthy/photo credit: Full Focus; pp 232–7: courtesy Loop. pH/photo credit: Loop.pH/Rachel Wingfield & Mathias Gmachl; pp 6, 166, 238–47: courtesy Marimekko/photo credit: Copyright Marimekko Corporation; pp 248–61: courtesy Nani Marquina/photo credit: Albert Font; pp 262–7: courtesy Nina Jobs/photo credits: Gärsnäs; Mathias Nero Stockholm, Collex Living Lapan, Nina Jobs, IKEA, David design, Windmill, Belle Maison Japan; pp 268–75: courtesy Inside/Outside; pp 276–83: courtesy Publisher Textiles/photo credits: Copyright Publisher Textiles 2007; pp 284–91: courtesy Sari Syväluoma/photo credits: Sari Syväluoma, Marte Garmann Johnsen, Per Erik Jæger, Espen Grønli, Fredrik Arff, Stina Glømmi; pp 292–7: courtesy Sophie Mallebranche; pp 5 (right), 165 (horizontal middle), 167 (horizontal), 298–311, 317: courtesy Timorous Beasties.

OPENER CAPTIONS: Page 5: (left to right) Alex Russell, Timorous Beasties; pages 6–7: (left to right) Maija Louekari, Alex Russell; page 9: (clockwise from bottom left) Hanna Werning, Alex Russell, Florence Manlik, Kahori Maki, c.neeon; pages 10–11: (left to right) Hanna Werning, Alex Russell, c.neeon, Kahori Maki; page 165: (top left) Camilla Diedrich, Helena Hietanen (top right), Timorous Beasties (middle), Johan Carpner (bottom right); pages 166–7: (clockwise from left) Maija Louekari, Johan Carpner, Timorous Beasties, Johan Carpner; page 313: (clockwise from top) Johan Carpner, Hanna Werning, Johan Carpner, c.neeon; page 315: Hanna Werning; page 317: Timorous Beasties.

AUTHOR'S ACKNOWLEDGMENTS

This book would not have been possible without the input of the 36 designers featured in it. I thank all of them for sharing their experience and inspirations, and for making this project interesting to research and a pleasure to write.

It seems like almost everyone I know shares my enthusiasm for the exciting new directions textiles are taking. Many were able to share their knowledge and contacts, and I especially appreciated the assistance I received from Reiko Sudo, Anne Kyyrö Quinn, Kahori Maki, Anne Toomey, Clare Johnston, Carole Collet, Carla Wachtveitl, Cabaret Aki, Jackal Kuzu, Natalie Chanin, Florence Müller, India Mahdavi, Maria Ben Saad and Laya Saludo Sweeney. A special thanks to Ingrid Giertz-Mårtenson and Jan Mårtenson, to whom this book is dedicated, for cheering me on while I wrote this and several of my previous books.

Last, but certainly not least, I'd like to thank the book's editors, Helen Evans and Zoe Antoniou, for their unwavering commitment to the project, and for all the fun we had along the way!